THE DUTCH IN THE SEVENTEENTH CENTURY

K.H.D. HALEY

with 158 illustrations, 18 in color

HARCOURT BRACE JOVANOVICH, INC.

For Ruth, Marian and Stephen

First American edition 1972

ISBN 0-15-126855-X *Hardbound*

ISBN 0-15-518473-3 *Paperbound*

Library of Congress Catalog Card Number: 72-157880

PRINTED AND BOUND IN GREAT BRITAIN BY JARROLD AND SONS LTD, NORWICH

CONTENTS

The interest of Englishmen, and of most Americans, in the history of seventeenth-century Europe has always tended to concentrate heavily on France. The long story of Anglo-French rivalry, the attractions of French literature, and the limited knowledge of most English-speaking people of any foreign language but French have combined to produce this result. Until comparatively recently Dutch history has suffered in comparison, except for the more dramatic episodes of the Revolt of the Netherlands. In the last forty years the work of Professor Geyl, Sir George Clark, Professor Wilson and Professor Boxer has done much to redress the balance, but this book has been written in the belief that there is still room for a general survey of Dutch society in its great age, and also in the conviction that no 'Library of European Civilization' could be without one.

It will be seen that my emphasis is different from that of Professor Wilson and Professor Boxer, though naturally I have had to make some reference to their fields of interest. I have been conscious of the inevitable limitations of space imposed by the form of the series of which this is part. Dutch society was such that there is almost no generalization about it to which some exception could not be found, and I hope that my Dutch friends will forgive me if, in trying to summarize its complexity and its variety, I have been guilty of some over-simplification, and (like Englishmen in the seventeenth century) have paid less attention than their due to some of its cities and some of its provinces.

I should like to record my thanks to all who helped in the preparation of this book; to Christopher Pick, to Erica Gentle and Constance Kaine and those other members of the staff of Thames and Hudson whose names I do not know but whose work I can appreciate, and to my typists at Sheffield University, Mrs Pat Holland and Miss Helen Pack.

NORTH SEA

VLIELAND

TEXEL

FRIESLAND

GRONINGEN

Groningen

DRENTHE

OVERIJSSEL

Hoorn

Enkhuizen

ZUIDER

Kampen

ZEE

Zwolle

Purmerend

Haarlem

Deventer

Amsterdam

HOLLAND

Leiden

UTRECHT

Utrecht

The Hague

Rijswijk

Delft

Gouda

Rotterdam

GELDERLAND

Waal

Dordrecht

Nijmegen

s'Hertogenbosch

ZEELAND

Veere

Breda

Tilburg

Middelburg

GENERALITY

Vlissingen

Bergen-
op-Zoom

LANDS

Maas

Rhine

N

0   50 Mls
0   80 Kms

Maastricht

1 The Dutch Republic in the seventeenth century.

THE UNION OF UTRECHT

In the cathedral city of Utrecht in 1579 the northernmost provinces of the Netherlands came together in a Union which developed into the Dutch Republic. Under the shadow of the great tower of the same Domkerk (though its nave had been ruined by a storm in the meantime), the diplomats of western Europe met in 1713 to conclude the War of the Spanish Succession with the Treaty of Utrecht. This was the fourth great peace conference in succession (following those of Breda, Nijmegen and Rijswijk) to meet on Dutch soil to settle the international problems of western Europe, so demonstrating the central position which the Dutch occupied in the power politics of the day; but in 1713, unlike the previous treaties, the essential decisions had been taken elsewhere, and ahead there now lay only a period of relative decline.

Between the Union of Utrecht and the Treaty of Utrecht only some four generations had elapsed. William III, whose horse stumbled in 1702, was actually the great-grandson of William the Silent, the 'father of his country'. A long-lived man, such as the versatile Constantijn Huygens (1596–1687), might live through nearly three-quarters of the period. But during these 134 years the Dutch, in proportion to the size of their population, made a contribution second to none to the development of European civilization. In politics they were at the core of the resistance, first of all to the domination of the Spanish Empire, and then to Louis XIV; they held their own for a time with England and gained the position of a great power. In the economic life of Europe they made themselves indispensable; their fleets of merchantmen and men-of-war sailed in every ocean, and no people was more prosperous. The artistic efflorescence of the 'Golden Age' was one of the most remarkable in all the history of painting. The degree of religious toleration which existed, though incomplete by modern standards, helped to demonstrate that uniformity of religious thought and practice was not essential to the coherence of a state, and that the ability to attract refugees from the intolerance of others could be a positive asset to the national life. The contribution of the Dutch to the intellectual life of Europe is less obvious, but important nonetheless. In many fields Dutch ideas and Dutch methods enjoyed the flattery of imitation – and that by some of the most progressive elements of European society. If the Dutch also had their share of jealousy and dislike from rivals, this too was in its way a tribute to their success.

It was a remarkable achievement. Yet in 1579, no one, not the most zealous of Dutch patriots or the keenest of foreign observers, could possibly have predicted it. Historians with the advantage of hindsight can detect that there were hidden advantages available for exploitation, but the most determined determinist would find it difficult to maintain that there was anything necessary, or even probable, about the success with which they were exploited.

It is true that the seventeen provinces of the Netherlands which Philip II of Spain had inherited in 1555 constituted one of the richest and most cultured parts of Europe; but the seven provinces which broke away were not the richest or the most populous part of the Netherlands. Their population, indeed, was then only about one and a half millions; at the height of their prosperity it cannot have amounted to much more than a third of the population of England, and, in proportion to France and to the Spanish Empire, it was much smaller even than that. In 1622 the population of the province of Holland, from which the Dutch derived over half their resources, amounted to some 672,000, perhaps twice the population of London alone; and the gap had probably been closed before the end of our period.

Manpower, to be sure, was not the vital consideration that it later became in the era of large national and industrialized states and total warfare. Governments with sufficient financial resources could enlist the services of foreign mercenaries; and in the land campaigns which occupied about two-thirds of the summers between 1579 and 1713 the Dutch armies did in fact contain a considerable proportion of Walloons, Frenchmen, Germans, English, and Scots – the 'Macs' who made a permanent career in the Dutch service, and the names of whose successors, we are told, are still to be found in Dutch telephone directories. In the navy the need to enlist foreigners was less, for, as will be seen, the proportion of the population which consisted of trained seamen was greater than in other states; but the use of the press-gang probably could not always have been avoided without the recruitment of sailors from Scandinavia and the north German ports. Yet the

2 The town hall at Utrecht where the delegates of the European powers met in 1713 to conclude the War of the Spanish Succession. The Domkerk towers behind the fishmarket (right).

armies and fleets which the Dutch deployed in a century of almost continuous war had to be paid, whether the men were natives or foreigners; but the country was so deficient in natural resources that it could not feed its own population, and had to seek the materials for its industries from elsewhere. Only the development of a remarkable financial and commercial expertise could remedy this.

There was another basic defect which had to be overcome. The seven provinces which adhered to the Union of Utrecht, in preference to the Union of Atrecht (or Arras) of the southern provinces which accepted Spanish rule, did not constitute any obvious natural unit. The frontier between rebel and Spanish-occupied territory did not correspond originally to any national, religious, social, historical or linguistic division. In an era when men thought that religious unity and political unity went hand in hand, the northern provinces contained at least as many Catholics as Protestants. The Union itself was a military alliance of seven very different provinces with different interests and strongly separatist instincts. It was essentially a defensive reaction against Spanish oppression, not the outcome of a positive Dutch national feeling which already existed. It was accompanied by no declaration of independence (the Act of Abjuration did not follow until 1581), and by no constitutional congress to plan the institutions of a new unitary state. The seven provinces did not all adhere to it at the same time; William the Silent himself did not accept the Union (which was largely the work of his brother, John of Nassau) for four months, his reluctance arising partly from some of its provisions and partly from his desire to maintain the unity of all the Netherlands, North and South. Neither rebels nor Spaniards wanted the Unions of Utrecht and Atrecht to bring into existence a permanent division of the country; while the Spaniards refused to concede independence to the North until 1648, many in the North retained hopes of freeing the South from Spanish rule until the 1630s. After all, there had been representatives of Flanders at Utrecht, and Ghent and Antwerp had officially adhered to the Union.

The Union was thus the product of a temporary alliance among seven provinces, Holland, Zeeland, Utrecht, Gelderland, Overijssel, Friesland and Groningen, to defend their local liberties; whether these provinces would coalesce to form a state or nation was a very different matter. They had both to struggle against the enmity of the mightiest empire of their day and to achieve a sufficient degree of internal

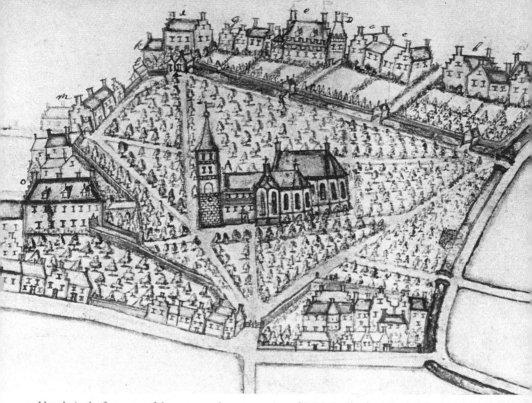

3 Utrecht in the first years of the seventeenth century: view of St John's church, with a canal and main street behind.

cohesion. In the decade after 1579 they alternately sought French help by acknowledging the Duke of Anjou as their protector, and English help by offering the sovereignty over the United Provinces to Queen Elizabeth. It was only experience that taught them that salvation must be achieved largely through their own efforts, rather than through putting themselves under the protection of an alternative foreign power to Spain. The following generation had to work out solutions to some of the most fundamental political problems.

THE SEA

To say that Dutch greatness began on the water is a commonplace, but it is nevertheless the indispensable starting-point. There were obvious reasons why the inhabitants of the seaward provinces should look to the water for a livelihood. The land of the provinces of Holland and

Zeeland in particular was low-lying, intersected by waterways and with larger expanses of lake and marsh than remain today. It was often easier to travel by boat than on horseback. As a result, the building-up of extensive landed estates with a dependent peasantry was a less easy and obvious form of social and economic organization here than elsewhere in Europe, while it made good sense to look for food in the form of fish, whether in rivers, lakes or the neighbouring North Sea.

The movement of the shoals of herring from the Baltic to the North Sea in the later Middle Ages, and the discovery of improved methods of salting and curing them, apparently by the Zeelander Beukels in the fourteenth century, stimulated the Dutch to exploit the riches of the North Sea by organizing the so-called Great Fishery. Not content merely with coastal fishing, they sailed from five ports in their *buizen* or 'busses', as contemporary Englishmen called them, and, starting in the Shetlands on St John's Day, 24 June, fished their way southwards, often within sight of the Scottish and English coasts (and arousing the same resentments as English fishermen have more recently done in Icelandic waters), until they reached the mouth of the Thames about the beginning of December. Unlike the English boats in the North Sea, which were often small and open and suitable only for short-distance fishing followed by salting on shore, the Dutch boats were specialized in construction; they were larger, they were decked, they

4 The fishmarket of Amsterdam.

5 *The Fishmarket at Leiden*, by Jan Steen, illustrates the importance of the fishing industry in Dutch prosperity.

carried salt on board and were able to wait for bigger catches while remaining economical to operate. It was even possible to pass the barrelled fish to other ships which carried the catch to harbour, leaving the busses to fish. Everything was carefully regulated by the 'College of the Fishery', and was based especially on the fishing-ports at the mouth of the river Maas.

Foreigners envious of the success of the Dutch fishing fleet, and more particularly English propagandists anxious to press their government to take action to secure the wealth of the sea for Englishmen, tended to exaggerate the scale and the value of this activity. One observer in about 1620 estimated that there were some 3,000 ships, manned by 50,000 men, fishing before the English coast. More recent research has tended to reduce these figures considerably, alleging that the highest number of ships reached, round the year 1600, was more like 500. But this in itself is a sufficiently impressive figure, particularly as it takes no account of boats fishing for cod, whether off the Dutch coast or on the Dogger Bank, or of the 200–250 whalers which sailed to the Arctic: between 1612 and 1641, a 'factory' was set up on the shores of Spitsbergen to deal with the carcasses of the whales which were slaughtered in large numbers. A contemporary thought that the fisheries were 'as lucrative as the mines of Peru'. A modern authority has estimated that if the value of the total annual catch of herring alone were conservatively estimated at two million pounds, this 'would put its national economic value at something roughly equivalent to the total export value of Britain's famous cloth industry.'

This plentiful supply of fish was one of the reasons why the Dutch were less vulnerable to the threat of famine than most other European countries; and the price was less apt to vary than the price of grain in times of bad harvests. But these large quantities of salted herring were by no means intended only for home consumption. They were exported both to the Baltic and to the Catholic countries of southern Europe, and were one of the commodities basic to the growth of Dutch overseas trade, leading Dutch seamen beyond their native North Sea. Moreover, they had to fetch the salt that they needed, and, since its quality was all-important, and North Sea and Scottish salt were insufficiently pure, they preferred to get it from the Bay of Bourgneuf on the Biscay shore of France, or, still further afield, from Setúbal in Portugal. And, since the Great Fishery was a seasonal business, both the men and the ships were available for this trade.

The origins both of this and of other branches of Dutch trade are clearly to be found before the Revolt. The Netherlands enjoyed certain obvious advantages from their geographical position; their ports had an important hinterland, both in their own cities, in one of the most highly urbanized parts of Europe, and in the Rhineland, and they were favourably placed for access at once to the Baltic and to Scandinavia, to the Thames and London, and to the Channel and the north and west of France.

Less obvious, perhaps, are the disadvantages which had to be overcome. There was virtually no timber for the construction of ships, and the shipbuilding industry which led Europe in quality and in technical progress in the seventeenth century was based on materials imported entirely from Norway and from the Baltic. Compared with Antwerp, London and Hamburg, the ports of the seven provinces

6 Hunting whales on the shores of Spitsbergen.

were poor. The great waterways which lead to modern Amsterdam and Rotterdam were essentially the work of the second half of the nineteenth century. Amsterdam itself was built on piles, and the shallowness of the water meant that the larger ships had to discharge by lighters. Sandbanks in the Zuider Zee and the narrowness of the entrance through the channel of the Vlie presented problems to sailing-ships. It was said that the journey from Amsterdam to the Texel was more dangerous than the whole of the rest of the journey to Spain.

At the beginning of the Revolt against Spain, therefore, Amsterdam was much inferior to Antwerp, which was nearer to the textile centres of the South. Nevertheless it already had some 30,000 inhabitants, and it enjoyed considerable prosperity, because through it came the vital supplies of grain which were needed for the cities of the Netherlands. The ships which brought the corn from Danzig by way of the Sound took part in what was called the 'mother trade', because this was, and remained until the eighteenth century, central to Amsterdam's prosperity. The records of the tolls levied by the kings of Denmark on shipping passing through the Sound show that all through the seventeenth century more than half the tonnage was Dutch, and of this a large proportion was owned in Amsterdam, whereas in Antwerp, great commercial centre though it had been, relatively few of the ships visiting the port were those of Antwerpers.

The decades of the 1560s and the 1570s, however, had on the whole been years of economic depression for the Netherlands. Between 1563 and 1570 the Sound was closed for long periods during a war between Denmark and Sweden, and between 1569 and 1573 the importation of unfinished cloth from England for finishing and re-export was stopped by the Duke of Alva. The outbreak of the Revolt in 1572 obviously led to economic dislocation; Amsterdam's prosperity suffered more than that of many places, not directly as a result of enemy action, but because of its delay in joining the rebel side. Only as a result of the *coup* known as the *Alteratie*, which overthrew the conservative and Catholic ruling oligarchy in 1578, did Amsterdam join the rest of Holland and Zeeland in opposition to Spain.

Thereafter circumstances suddenly favoured the growth of Amsterdam and the other ports of the North. While the trade of Antwerp was severely handicapped by the activities of privateers at the mouth of the river Scheldt and by the havoc of the Spanish and French 'furies', Amsterdam, after 1578, was unhampered by nearby military operations or by the activities of mutinous troops. Finally, in 1585, after a damaging siege lasting a year, Antwerp was recovered for Spain by Philip II's Governor-General, the Duke of Parma. At first the loss of this great city seemed a disaster to the cause of the Dutch rebels, but it proved to have more than merely compensating advantages for the cities of the North. Securely reoccupied and garrisoned by Spanish troops, Antwerp never recovered its former greatness. The Zeeland privateers effectively kept the river Scheldt closed to foreign shipping. Not only did foreign traders transfer their interests to the ports of the North, but many inhabitants of Antwerp and the cities of the South preferred to move northwards to new homes. Permitted to sell their possessions and emigrate by the agreements which Parma himself made with many of the provinces and cities of the South, they moved not only to escape from a detested Spanish rule and to be able to worship in their own way, but because cities like Amsterdam and Rotterdam now seemed to offer greater economic opportunities; thus a Catholic like Johan van der Veken could emigrate and become a

7 Model of a mid-seventeenth-
century *fluyt*: economical and
well designed, the *fluyt* gave the
Dutch a significant trading
advantage.

financial adviser to the leading Dutch statesman, Jan van Oldenbarnevelt. Such merchants took with them a knowledge of the most
advanced financial and commercial techniques in Europe, and, though
naturally they did not create a commercial life where none had
existed before, they were, to say the least, a useful reinforcement in
Middelburg, Rotterdam and particularly in Amsterdam.

At almost the same time Dutch merchants and sailors received an
important competitive advantage from the building of the famous
fluyts, or 'fluteships'. Apparently first developed in Hoorn about the
year 1590, they represented an important advance on anything previously possessed either by the Dutch or by anyone else. Though the
timber for the shipyards of Amsterdam and the river Zaan had to be
fetched from Norway or the Baltic, the *fluyt* was, in the first place,
considerably cheaper to construct. As late as 1676 it was calculated
that an English ship of 250 tons cost £7.2s.6d. per ton, while one
bought from Zaandam cost £4.10s. per ton. This was partly the

8 Building ships for the East India trade.

result of the development of what was for those days relatively large-
scale and standardized production, with the aid of labour-saving
machinery – cranes for handling heavy timber, and, most important,
wind-driven sawmills. But it was also the result of technical pro-
ficiency and skill in the design of the ships. The Dutch led the way in
the design of all kinds of vessel – from warships to the fast-sailing
jacht, whose name was adopted into the English language – but it was
in purpose-built cargo ships that their dominance was most important.

Though it made its appearance in time of war, the *fluyt* embodied
for the first time a differentiation between the functions of the mer-
chantman and the ship of war. With a flat bottom and shallow draught
which betrayed its derivation from the barges which sailed the inland
waterways, the *fluyt* was little more than a closed hold. It had a length
from four to six times its beam; and its masts were as far apart as
possible to allow room for a big main hold. Moreover, because it

9, 10 Two Dutch ships: the *fluyt* (above) and the fast–sailing *jacht* (below).

carried few or no guns, because the rigging was relatively simple and because winches or tackles were used wherever possible, it needed a smaller crew and was much more economical to run. A Dutch ship of 200 tons might therefore need only ten men, while an English ship of the same size might carry as many as thirty. If it is true, in addition, that wages were lower and provisioning cheaper, the combined effect was to allow the Dutch to offer freight rates a third to a half lower than those, for instance, of their English competitors in the seventeenth century.

Developed during the 1590s, and produced in particularly large numbers during the Twelve Years' Truce with Spain between 1609 and 1621, with refinements to cater for specialized cargoes like timber, the *fluyt* carried all before it in northern European waters; other countries often found it more convenient to buy Dutch ships than to build their own. At the same time, during the last decade of the sixteenth century, Dutch sailors also extended their scope to other seas. This was no doubt the outcome of a great surge of enterprise and self-confidence, but it also showed the ability to turn temporary circumstances to account. After some years of vacillation, wondering whether an embargo might do more harm to his own subjects than to the Dutch rebels, Philip II finally decided to close the ports of Spain and Portugal to them; but this only stimulated the Dutch to seek to trade directly with the Mediterranean. Steven van der Haghen pioneered the extension of the older *Westvaart* into a *Straatvaart* through the Straits of Gibraltar. The Dutch found that their desire for Mediterranean produce coincided with the desperate need of Italy in particular for additional food supplies. The early 1590s were years of bad harvests there, as elsewhere in western Europe, and the arrival of Dutch ships bringing grain from the expanding areas of production in Poland was extremely convenient.

It was said that no less than 200 ships carried grain through the Straits in the autumn of 1591. It was not long before a Dutch consul was established at the Tuscan port of Leghorn, and soon the newcomers were exploiting all the commercial possibilities of trade between Italian ports as well as between the Netherlands and Italy. One of the commodities brought back from Leghorn was marble, and it was eventually in Amsterdam, not in the Italian quarries themselves, that Louis XIV found it convenient to buy the marble that he needed for his palace at Versailles. Within a few years the Dutch

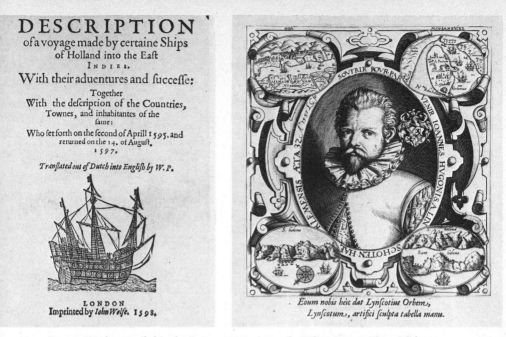

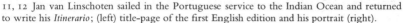

11, 12 Jan van Linschoten sailed in the Portuguese service to the Indian Ocean and returned to write his *Itinerario*; (left) title-page of the first English edition and his portrait (right).

received French assistance to persuade the Sultan to allow them to trade to Constantinople; their reputation as enemies of Spain was one factor which induced the Turks to encourage them, and in 1612 an agreement was negotiated which gave them the right to trade in the whole of the Ottoman Empire. Consuls were established in the main ports, and particularly in Smyrna.

Philip II's attempt to close the ports of Portugal, including the salt supplies of Setúbal, to his hated rebel subjects was one reason why they also ventured across the Atlantic to seek salt on the shores of Venezuela. But the Caribbean and the mainland of South America also offered other opportunities. The plantations there needed ships to import slaves and to take away their sugar; and in spite of all that Philip could do it seems that a good deal of Brazilian sugar was conveyed to Europe in Dutch vessels even before, in the third decade of the seventeenth century, the Dutch formed the ambition to conquer Brazil for themselves. Further north they established themselves in Guiana, and in Curaçao and other islands close to the Spanish Main. Elsewhere across the oceans, however, there was a greater temptation to break into the areas in the East Indies from which the Portuguese imported valuable spices. Desire for gain and the wish to strike another blow against Philip II fortunately coincided, and the geographer and Calvinist theologian, Petrus Plancius, joined with merchant backers to find a way there. Attempts to discover a north-east passage met an icy end, and the endeavour to use the Straits of Magellan was no more successful, though between 1598 and 1601 Olivier van der Noort became the first Dutch sea-captain to sail round the world.

Soon, however, the Dutch discovered the secrets of the route to the Spice Islands by way of the Cape of Good Hope, with the aid of Jan van Linschoten, who had served under the Archbishop of Goa before returning home and publishing his *Itinerario* in 1597. The first voyage backed by an Amsterdam syndicate was not a financial success, but in July 1599 part of the second fleet under van Neck arrived home after an absence of fourteen and a half months, carrying 600,000 pounds of pepper, and 250,000 pounds of cloves, together with nutmeg and mace. 'For as long as Holland has been Holland, there have never arrived ships as richly laden as these', said an anonymous contemporary. All the church bells of Amsterdam rang in celebration of this 'Happy Return', and those who had raised the capital of 800,000 florins received a profit of 100 per cent, with some of the ships still to return.

After much persuasion the various companies which sprang up in different ports to exploit this lucrative trade were combined by the

13 Jan Coen, first Governor-General of the Dutch East Indies Company and founder of the port of Batavia in Java.

14 *Landscape in Brazil* by Frans Post, court painter to Johan Maurits of Nassau-Siegen, Governor of the Dutch Brazilian territories from 1637 to 1644.

statesman Oldenbarnevelt into the famous Dutch East Indies Company which received its charter from the States-General in 1602. Six and a half million florins of capital were rapidly subscribed – before a penny had been paid in, the shares were selling on the Amsterdam Exchange at a premium of 15 per cent – and the new company pressed on with a vigour much greater than that shown by its contemporary English rival. In the first seven years of its existence the Dutch company sent fifty-five great ships, while in nine years the English sent twelve. Using a more direct route from the Cape of Good Hope to the Straits of Sunda, which avoided the need to follow the coast of East Africa and strike across the Indian Ocean to Goa as the Portuguese had done, the newcomers soon found themselves able to break up the position which the Portuguese had occupied for the past century. It is no part of the plan of this book to describe in detail the process by which, under the inspiration of governors-general like Coen, a new Batavia was

founded in Java, from which the riches of the Indonesian archipelago could be exploited; but in the course of their journeys to Batavia the East Indiamen came within sight of the barren coast of western Australia, while to the north Dutch sailors and merchants reached Japan, and, through the Straits of New Guinea, Tasman penetrated into waters beyond the east coast of Australia.

Spectacular as the Dutch success in the East Indies obviously was, it is necessary to keep it in proportion. Neither in the number of ships involved (though the East Indiamen were undoubtedly the largest), nor in the amount of capital invested, was the East India trade equal to that with the Mediterranean in the seventeenth century, and it fell far short of Amsterdam's 'mother-trade' to the Baltic. Nevertheless the profits were such as to arouse the envy of Europe. It seemed as if

15 Painted chart of Amboina, Indonesia, dating from 1617: at the bottom right is a portrait of the first Governor, Frederik de Hartman.

16 The characteristically dressed Dutch merchant and his wife suggest that Aelbert Cuyp's painting of the East Indies fleet in the bay of Batavia was a work of the imagination: Cuyp himself never left Holland.

17 View of the small Dutch settlement of New Amsterdam, founded in 1625–26, from a map

the trade-routes, not merely of Europe but of all the continents, were being made to meet in the Netherlands, and particularly at Amsterdam. Dutch sailors left a permanent mark on the map of the world: from Spitsbergen to Cape Hoorn, and from Brooklyn to New Zealand, the geographical names given by them are still in use. Indeed, for many decades the maps themselves were generally Dutch. The charts of Lucas van Wagenaer, published in the *Spieghel van Zeevaert* in 1584, rapidly commended themselves to the sailors of other nations too. An English version, the *Mariner's Mirrour*, was published in 1588, and, anglicized as 'Waggoners', Wagenaer's charts were in general use. The Dutch publishers, Blaeu and Hondius, led the way in the production of more general maps and atlases in the seventeenth century.

18 Dutch place-names in America: this detail of Claes Visscher's map of North America

of North America by Claes Visscher.

    Precise statistics about the numbers of Dutch ships are impossible to obtain. As in the case of fishing-vessels, they were naturally exaggerated by foreign publicists and politicians who wished their own rulers to take appropriate action. But it has recently been suggested that, by 1670, the volume of Dutch-owned shipping may have been something like 568,000 tons, and that it may have considerably exceeded that of Spanish, Portuguese, French, English, Scottish and German shipping combined. Professor Boxer has adopted the figure of 80,000 Dutch sailors as a reasonable estimate, and this, if correct, would be the equivalent of at least 10 per cent of the adult male population – though the figure includes men of other nationalities attracted into the Dutch service. On their efforts Dutch prosperity

clearly shows Long Island (t Lange Eylandt), Staten Island and Brooklyn (Breukelen).

ultimately rested, and it is well to remember the privations that they had to undergo in the interests of the prosperity of the people of the cities of Holland and Zeeland. They had to contend not only with the buffetings of wind and sea, with the dangers of pirates and sale into slavery, and with scurvy and dysentery, but with low wages, bad food and ferocious discipline.

Descriptions of the way in which crews were recruited by shipping masters or by agents known as 'cats and dogs', and accounts of the conditions on the East Indiamen in the long and tedious months of their passages, make exceedingly grim reading; it is not surprising that many men were brutalized by the way in which they had to live and work, or that when opportunity offered they sought relief in drink and women. On the other hand, there is no reason to suppose that conditions in Dutch ships were worse than those in others; it is even possible that Dutch habits of cleanliness may have made them slightly better on the long voyages. Certainly these conditions were everywhere regarded as natural and normal at the time, and did not deter foreigners from seeking a livelihood there in preference to their own countries. And if those who stayed at home did not fully appreciate them, it is true even today that the price, in terms of human discomfort, of fish from northern waters is still commonly forgotten.

The sea-routes which were the Dutch lifeline obviously needed armed protection. The Dutch had not only to be efficient and enterprising at sea, but had to make themselves formidable. At the beginning of the Revolt against Spain, when indeed there was still no clear distinction between men-of-war and merchantmen, there was nothing in the shape of a national fleet. Privateers, on the other hand, there were, preying especially on Spanish shipping with or without letters of marque granted by the Prince of Orange, and the so-called Sea Beggars, animated by a mixture of greed for loot, hatred of Spanish rule, and Calvinist extremism – *Liever Turcx dan Paus* (better Turk than Pope) was their motto – wrought considerable havoc. They could never be described as a disciplined force. In 1573, however, Dutch ships defeated the Spanish admiral Bossu off Hoorn in the Zuider Zee, and thereafter the primary task of controlling the local water against the forces of Philip II was safely under control: in 1588 Dutch ships operating off the coasts of Flanders helped to ward off the danger of a junction between the forces of the Duke of Parma and the Spanish Armada, and there is a sense in which the defeat of the Armada

19 The Sea Beggars capture Brill in April 1572, a first step in the revolt against Spanish rule.

20 *Liever Turcx dan Paus*,
example of a propaganda badge
worn by the Sea Beggars.

21 Medal struck at Middelburg
to commemorate the defeat
of the Spanish Armada.

22 The battle of Gibraltar, in which the Dutch inflicted a severe defeat on the Spanish fleet.

23 Tromp's victory off the Downs: a pen and ink drawing by Willem van de Velde the Elder.

was a Dutch victory as well as an English one. Thereafter, privateers operating chiefly from the ports of Zeeland not only closed the Scheldt to all shipping but went much further afield in search of prizes – an obvious attraction for investment as long as the war with Spain lasted.

It rapidly became clear, however, that a more organized fleet was necessary. The more unarmed herring-busses and flutes were used, the more reliance had to be placed on convoys to protect them from enemy privateers, operating especially from Dunkirk and Ostend. In 1597, therefore, the States-General set up five admiralties in the sea-provinces to deal with naval administration, and this organization, cumbersome as it was, concerned itself with the fitting-out of fleets for destinations near and far. In 1607 van Heemskerck's victory off Gibraltar was a sign that Dutch armed might, as well as grain ships, had appeared in the Mediterranean, and thereafter there were frequent expeditions against the Barbary pirates. In 1639 Tromp won an even more startling victory over the Spaniards in the Downs, in waters which the English considered their own, and which were

T EYLANT CUBA MET SYNE GELEGEN'THEYT

24 A contemporary print depicts the capture of the silver fleet off Cuba: top left and right are portraits of Hein and Admiral Hendrick; a map of Cuba completes the picture.

indeed within sight of the English coast. Elsewhere, Dutch fleets soon appeared in the Baltic to assist Dutch state policy in preventing any power from obtaining too tight control over the vital passage through the Sound and in avoiding any recurrence of the great economic dislocation which had attended the Baltic war of 1563–70 and the cutting-off of the Polish grain supplies. Still further afield, the fleets of the West India Company (founded in 1621 to attack the Spanish-Portuguese position in the Caribbean and Brazil) were more successful than those of Drake, Hawkins and Raleigh, and in 1628 Piet Hein achieved the dream of many a sea-dog, and became one of the permanent heroes of Dutch folk-lore, when he captured the Spanish silver fleet off the coast of Cuba, with treasure amounting to 15 million florins.

These victories, and the later successes of Tromp, de Ruyter and others, were partly the outcome of superior seamanship, and partly the result of greater shipbuilding skill. The Dutch led the way in warships as in merchantmen, to the extent that other states in search of them went to Amsterdam to buy them: in 1628–29 Richelieu's fleet was of Dutch origin, and in the war between Sweden and

25 Piet Hein.

26 The West India House at Amsterdam, headquarters of the Company which dispatched Piet Hein's expedition.

Denmark in 1644–45 the fleets of both powers had been fitted out in Amsterdam by the great Dutch entrepreneurs, de Geer and Marcellis respectively. In 1666 Colbert, much as he detested Dutch strength at sea, found himself commissioning two ships at Zaandam and two at Amsterdam. But there was another factor which helps to explain the way in which the Dutch held their own against other navies. For their commanders they relied neither on converted army officers nor on gentleman volunteers. Some admirals, like Wassenaer-Opdam, had noble origins, but others, like Hein, the Tromps, de Ruyter and the Evertsens, either came from humble families or were the sons of sailors and spent a lifetime at sea.

The greatest of the Tromps was only eight when he sailed with his father, who commanded a frigate at the battle of Gibraltar. He spent two and a half years in slavery in North Africa after being captured by an English pirate, and saw thirty or forty years of service before he was killed in 1653 and buried at Delft in the same church as the princes of Orange, with a splendid monument to his memory. De Ruyter spent his boyhood in a ropewalk at Flushing and always preserved the sober, unpretentious manners of his Zeeland upbring-

27 Tromp's monument in the Oude Kerk, Delft.

28 Admiral Michiel de Ruyter, pictured in a domestic setting with his wife and other members of his family.

ing. A French officer was startled to observe how, immediately after the Four Days' Battle of 1666, the Admiral took up a broom, started to clean his cabin, and then went out to feed his chickens. Except when being drawn by Bol or Blooteling, he always wore 'the clothes of the commonest sea-captain'; the English ambassador commented on the simplicity of his way of life, saying that he was accompanied through the streets by only one servant. He was pious, sober, and 'careful' with his money; his wife went out every day with her servants, carrying the provision basket and buying food in the market like any burgher's wife, and did the household washing herself, hanging the clothes on the line in the attic.

Both Tromp and de Ruyter were known to their sailors as 'Bestevaer' (Grandad), a nickname which it is difficult to imagine being bestowed upon their contemporaries in other fleets. Social distinctions were less of an obstacle to merit; it was easier to reach the top and, perhaps, to command loyalty – though under the conditions of sea battles at that time every failure was liable to be followed by recriminations among the officers, particularly if they were divided by political considerations.

29 Windmill used in the drainage of the Beemster polder.

ECONOMIC LIFE

If the Dutch depended on the willingness of their sailors to fetch goods from the end of the world, and on their fighting ability to keep the sea-lanes open, it is equally true that the sailors could have achieved nothing without the existence of a relatively large class of people with capital to invest in overseas trade, a keen eye for possibilities of profit and the intelligence to make the best use of the most up-to-date financial techniques. Though there were undoubtedly some very large-scale investors and entrepreneurs, the availability of capital for investment was fairly widely diffused. There was, moreover, little outlet for it in the purchase of land, unless it was in the drainage of polders like the Beemster, which reflected the rise in property values near the rapidly growing city of Amsterdam. There was every incentive to turn to some form of commercial enterprise, and it was normal both for ships to be part-owned (with some active and some sleeping partners), and for the ships to be chartered in whole or in part by others, instead of carrying merely the cargoes of the owners. The result was a reduction of risks, competitive and relatively low freight charges, and constant pressure on ships in foreign ports to seek return cargoes.

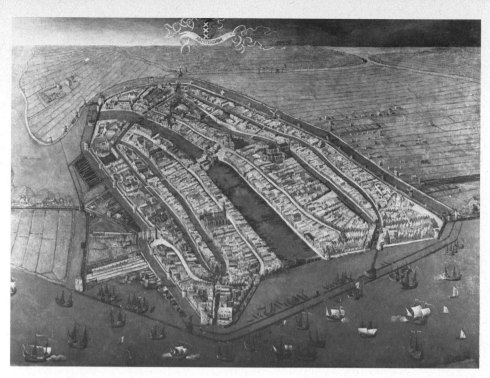

30, 31 Cornelis Anthonisz's painting of Amsterdam in 1536 (above) and a plan of the city from 1663 (below) reveal the rapid expansion of Amsterdam.

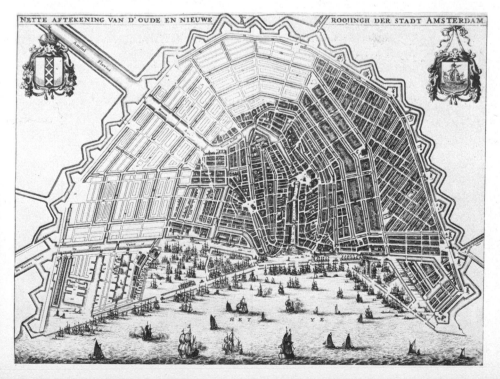

Both capital and energy were also injected by the refugees whom Parma permitted to leave Antwerp and the cities of the South, taking with them their wealth and looking eagerly for new opportunities. William Usselincx, the zealous propagandist of a West India Company to break open the Spanish monopoly of the New World, Johan van der Veken, Isaac Lemaire and Balthasar de Moucheron were some of the best-known names. There were failures as well as successes: Moucheron, the son of a French Huguenot nobleman whose ships all carried the Moucheron colours, a Burgundy cross on a green field, eventually went bankrupt after voyages in search of the north-east passage, to West Africa and to both West and East Indies. It would be wrong to attribute too much even to those Southerners who were successful (or to the Sephardic Jews who came from the Iberian peninsula at about the same time); Dutch capitalism was widely based. Yet they must have helped to stimulate enterprise, making use of their old trading connections, particularly with southern Europe, and to spread the financial techniques which had flourished in Antwerp after originating in the Mediterranean.

The Dutch were not remarkable for many innovations, but rather for the more effective and intensive use of methods already known elsewhere. Marine insurance was not new; what was significant was that by the 1590s printed forms were employed for the purpose in Amsterdam, and that in 1598 a municipal ordinance set up a chamber of assurance to register policies and settle disputes. By 1635 the premiums were estimated at over 400,000 florins annually, and during the second Anglo-Dutch war of the 1660s enemy shipping was insured at Amsterdam. Printed forms of bills of exchange were also in use by the 1590s, and in 1598 a Rotterdam financier named Wissel took the first initiative towards setting up a bank, on Italian principles, which would facilitate the deposit and transfer of money, while avoiding the problems connected with the defective coins of the day.

Wissel's own schemes failed, but in 1609 the famous Bank of Amsterdam was set up with municipal backing. It was not the first public bank – Venice had introduced one in 1587 – but its success was on a far larger scale, and it helped to make Amsterdam the principal money market in Europe for nearly two centuries. Within two years there were 708 depositors, and by 1701 there were 2,698, with deposits amounting to more than 16 million florins. The Bank's reputation became so solid that it survived without strain the acute political

32 The cornmarket at Amsterdam.

crisis of 1672, when French troops almost reached the gates of Amsterdam and there were riots against de Witt's régime. Dutch and foreign merchants found in Amsterdam unequalled exchange and insurance facilities, ease of payment and opportunities for the investment of their gains.

The result was an expanding fund of credit and lower rates of interest in the Netherlands than elsewhere, and this was to the advantage not only of private borrowers but also of the state. It is remarkable that in a time of war, when the state's debt was doubling, Oldenbarnevelt was able to boast of reducing the interest on it from 12 to $6\frac{1}{4}$ per cent, and eventually, in 1655, de Witt converted the debt to 4 per cent. When it is recalled that in the England of Charles II the legal rate of interest was 6 per cent and that the government had to pay 'allowances' on top of this, it is easy to see that the cheap supply of money was at the root of Dutch power as well as Dutch economic prosperity. Other rulers, indeed, sometimes found it convenient to use the facilities of the Amsterdam money market: James I and Richelieu sent subsidies to their allies in Germany by way of Amsterdam; both parties in the English Civil War sought credit there; and the emperors borrowed money there on the security of their quicksilver mines.

Many purely financial transactions took place on the new Amsterdam Bourse, first used in 1611. One feature which does seem to have been new was the growth of speculation in East India Company

Smack de Port a Port	100	16 a 18		15
Engels Coper-root		620	gl	5
Dito Sweedts			gl	
Roomsen Aluyn		40		
Dito Luycksen Aluyn		37 a 38		15
Dito Engelse Aluyn	100 ℔	35 a 36		15

Nᵒ.4.   Droegen by 't ℔. Contant

Quickfilver ℔ 36		Cinabrio 38		
Boraso raf. ℔ 25 a 26		Seduw. fijn 10		15
Rob fijn 50 t a 8 gl		Benju. fijn 24 a 60		15
Turbit 80		Manna 24 a 32		
Salarm. 10 a 11 ℔ 8		Mastien 30		15
Seservat 24 a 43		Lange Peper 4,8 a 8		15
Cassa Linge 15 a 16		Senebla. 16 a 18 a 48		15
Salse Parille 43		Opoponare 44		15
Coloquinta ℔ 28 a 30		Cardemom 38 a 40		15
Wit. Wierook ℔ 8 a 16		Mechoacan 16 a 40		15
Coculus ℔ 19		Gom Trag. ℔ 12 a 13		15
Corc. 100 ℔ 28 a 40		Galanga 46		15
Bittere Amandelen 't 100 ℔		45	gl	
Camfer rafinato 48		Cassa Fistula 40	gl	
Sap van Soethout 't 100 ℔		30 a 34	gl	
Irias 't 100 ℔ 30 gl		Kubebe ℔ 19		15
Terbentina venet 't 100 ℔		40 a 46	gl	
Scamonium		℔ 7 a 8	gl	

By 't Ons

Befar steen Orient 14 a 18		Dito Occid. 66	15
Ambre Grifs 66		Moschus 10 a 17 a 22	gl
Stamp Peerlen 36 a 42		15 a 6 a 10	gl
Amsterdams oprecht Civet		16	gl

**Amsterdamse Goude Leppen / gemaeckt
door Hans le Maire. d'Elle**

Verheven Nieuw inventie		54	15
Dito Geamaileerde		56	15
Extra geschilderte bloemen		88	15

Nᵒ.5.   Talck Traen en Stockvis 't 100 ℔

Oosters Talck	20 a 21	gl	c
Soeten Talck	22	gl 10	c
Moscovise Talck	18 a 20	gl	c
Lever Traen	18 a 19	gl	t
Groenlantse Traen			
Speck-traen	37,10 a 38	gl	c
Robbe Traen	37 a 38	gl	c
Inlantse Traen, de Ton	26	gl	c
Eylantse Walvis Baerden	65 a 67	gl	
Rontvis	10,5 a 10	gl	10
Rootschaer	8 a 9	gl	
Lenge	10 a 11	gl	
Yslantse Vis	9,10 a 9	gl	15

Nᵒ.6.1   Honigh - Contant

Bordense Honigh 't vat	40 a 41		℔
Bajoensen Honigh 100 ℔	10 a 10	gl	10
Honigh van Breta 100 ℔	12 a 13	gl	
Bremer Honigh de Ton	35 a 36	gl	
Inlantse Honigh de Ton	37 a 38	gl	
Nantese Honigh	12,10 a 13	gl	

Nᵒ.7.   Olyen by 't Vat en by de Aem. Cont.

Genuase Oly 60 a 67	Dito Poelse 57		℔
dito Civielse	dito Portug. 48 a 52		℔
Malgomse	Majorcj 52		
Lijn Oly 34	gl	Raep Oly 37	gl

Van 12 a 13 a 33 a 13 a 18	Van 16 a 17 ℔		13
Spaens-Leer van 24 ℔ 't Dozijn 32 a 33			℔
Idem 17 a 18 ℔	32		
Oosters 22 a 24 ℔ 24 a 26 ℔ Idem 15 a 18 ℔ 22 a 23			
Sool-Leer van 25 a 26 ℔	12 a 12		℔
Idem 18 a 20 ℔	11,8 a 12		℔

Nᵒ.10.   Spaense Wijnen. Contant.

Serese Secken 't vat N 40 a 50			℔
Piere Semijn Wijn N 40 a 46			℔
Canary-wijn	a		℔

Franse Wijnen.   Contant

Petouwen Stom	℔	Wijn	℔
Conjacken Schoon	a		℔
Bordeuse	S	a	℔
Langonse Wijnen	S	a	℔
Libornse	S	a	℔
Hooghlamtse wijn	S	a	℔
Nantese	S	a	℔
Nantse Brandew. 30 vier.			℔
Conjackse	a		℔
Bord. Brandewijn			℔
Bier Brandewijn. De Aem 48			gl
Koorn Brandewijn. De Aem 44			gl

Nᵒ.11.   Tin/ Loot en Was. Contant.

Engels Loot	26 a 27		15
Bronswijck Loot	26		15 6
Engels block Tin	52		gl
Fijn duytsch kufz Tin	52		gl
Slachwalder kufz Tin	52		gl
Oldenburger kufz Tin	50		gl
Amsterdams proef Tin	52		gl
Franckforder proef Tin	45		gl
Klaer Tin	38		gl
Inlandts Was, met 100 ℔ 72 a 73			gl
Droog Oost. Was, 100 ℔ 71 a 73			gl
Gemeen Oosters 100 ℔ 68			gl
Oosters Ver-Was 100 ℔ 60			gl

Nᵒ.12.   Wolle.

Segovia gesort. de prim. 31 a 33 a 36			℔
Sooria 26 a. 8 a 29 Soria Seg. 30 a 32			℔
Petite Seg. gesort prim. 26 a 27			℔
Mol. en Cast. gesort de pri. 22 a 24			℔
Alber. Wol 'e pri. 27 ℔ Pet. Alb. a			stl
Sevilise gesorteert de pri. 19 a 20			℔
Seg. Lam. wolle 100 ℔ 60 a 65 a 70			gl
Mol. Cast. en Aelb Lam w. 45 a 50			gl tij
Pomer ingeb. wol 100 ℔ 31 a 32	gl		m. r
dito Fijne gryse 100 ℔ 39	gl		cont
Rostocker 100 ℔ 33			m. r
Stettijnse 100 ℔ 30 a 33	gl		m. r
Dantzicker 100 ℔ 30 a 31	gl		m. r
Poolfse Lam. Wolle van 14 a 28			m. r
Dito Somer Wolle van 12 a 14 ℔ 15			m. r
Lun. en Bre. schoor 100 ℔ 24 a 46 gl			15 m. r
Rijnse ingebond. 100 ℔ 26 a 28 gl			cont
Dito Uytgebond. 100 ℔ 35 a 37 gl			con
Halb. en Duringer 100 ℔ 42 a 43 gl			con
Rijnsse Pel-Wolle 100 ℔ 27 a 30 gl			con

34, 35 Industries of Holland: glass-blowing and diamond-cutting.

shares or 'actions'. In 1609, within a few years of the issue of shares, Isaac Lemaire and a group of bears made a systematic attempt to depress their price for their own advantage, and this was only the prelude to the appearance of brokers, playing the market. But Amsterdam also became the foremost commodity market in Europe. Not far from the Bourse were the warehouses storing Polish grain, Swedish copper, Spanish wool, American tobacco, Brazilian sugar, East Indian spices. Commodity price lists were printed from the 1580s and used throughout western Europe; in 1634 there were 359 different price quotations, and in 1686, 550. From trading in actual goods in the warehouses it was a natural step to go on to trade in futures. One special form of trading which deserves mention is that in arms and munitions of every kind, based on connections with the foundries of the bishopric of Liège, and copper and iron supplies from Sweden and elsewhere. Cannon and gunpowder were supplied with complete impartiality to allies, neutrals and enemies, and Amsterdam was still one of the main munitions markets of Europe in the time of the War of the Austrian Succession.

Some of these commodities were imported only to be re-exported in the same state, paying only low duties. Others, however, became

◀ 33 A commodity price list of 1674 quotes prices in Spanish and French wines, tallow, cloth, honey and tin.

36 Washing fleeces and sorting wool: from a painting by Isaac Swanenburgh.

the materials for Dutch industries, for the cities of Holland were industrial as well as commercial communities. The shipbuilding industries of the Zaanstreek and Amsterdam, using imported timber, have already been mentioned, and to these can be added ropewalks and other ancillary crafts. But there were also soap-boiling, sugar-refining, the curing of tobacco, glass-blowing, diamond-cutting (taken over from Antwerp), and many others, all carried out in workshops and using raw materials, or half-finished ones, from abroad. There was a linen industry at Haarlem, where there were good natural facilities for bleaching, and silk at Amsterdam. And there was a great spurt in the textile industry at Leiden.

Leiden had long been a centre for the manufacture of cloth, but until after the Revolt this had been in a state of decline. The dwindling market for the older and heavier types of cloth, the loss of supplies of English wool, financial weakness, a devotion to tradition and a disinclination to experiment with new methods and cloths, and, finally, civil unrest culminating in the great siege of 1574, all led to depression, declining production and poverty. At the time of the siege the population, augmented by refugees from the surrounding villages, amounted to about 12,500. But within a few years of the great victory against Spain there was a new spirit abroad and a new confidence, encouraged by the return of some Calvinist refugees from Colchester and by a much larger group from Hondschoote in Flanders. The latter came from an area which had suffered severely from the fighting. They came at first in a body, not individually, making conditions with the city authorities and bringing with them the skill to make new and lighter types of cloth; and they were followed by many others. In a quarter of a century the total cloth production of Leiden doubled, and by 1622 the population was over 40,000. Much of this was due to the stimulus provided by the immigrants from Flanders, of whom some 3,600 heads of families were admitted to the *poorterschap*, without reckoning other members of families and those who were too poor to seek the freedom of the city. It is right also to pay tribute to the enlightenment of the civic authorities, who, like those in other Dutch cities, saw what was to be gained by the humane encouragement of immigration under easy conditions. Production and population went on to reach a peak in 1671, and Leiden may even have become the largest industrial city in Europe with the exception of Lyons.

As in the case of the sailors who manned the ships, industrial growth was won at the price of terrible conditions for those who laboured. Hours were long, indirect taxation bore heavily, housing was inadequate, and it was said that in Leiden there were 'more beggars than in the whole of the rest of Holland'. In 1622 a quarter of the population was excused payment of the poll-tax for reasons of poverty, and in 1634 some 20,000 received a distribution of bread. The sweated labour of men was augmented by that of women and children, some of whom were brought from Liége and given light work from the ages of 6 and 7, heavier work from 15. Sometimes attempts were made by the magistrates to set up inspectors and prevent the ill-treatment of children, and, as will be seen, the Dutch cities gave more relief to the poor than anywhere else in Europe; but the picture of these early modern industrial conditions remains a grim one.

Many contemporaries were critical and contemptuous of the Dutch greed for gain – not, however, because of the hardships it meant for the poor, which everyone took for granted, but because they held the traditional view that commercial activity was inseparable from

37 View of Enkhuizen and its agricultural lands about 1600.

avarice, and scorned to work in the counting-house. Some avarice there undoubtedly was, and it would be easy to illustrate it by repeating the well-known story of the sea-captain who is alleged to have remarked that he would sail through hell until the sails of his boat were singed if there were profit at the end of it. A better example, because it was widespread as well as based on fact, is the well-known Dutch practice of trading with the enemy in war-time. Though notions of contraband and blockade were very different from those of today, contemporaries were surprised by the systematic way in which the Dutch continued to trade with Spain without serious official disapproval, and when the Earl of Leicester came over with English assistance in 1585 he tried, quite ineffectually, to get it banned.

There was, indeed, a strong case for arguing that the trade would be more helpful in building up Dutch commercial and financial strength than a ban would be harmful to Spain; but sometimes this was little more than a rationalization of self-interest, and it would

be hard to extend it to cover the supplies of powder, match and lead to the armies of Louis XIV for their war with the Dutch in 1672–78. Yet it would be difficult to assert that the rapacity of the Dutch merchants was in general worse than that of aristocrats in other countries who sought to extend their estates, landlords who rack-rented and evicted their tenants, royal favourites greedy for pensions and financial privileges, or lawyers who demanded large fees at the bar. The satirical comments of English critics were directed at a particular kind of greed, and in this they reflected the prejudices of an aristocratic and landed society, compounded sometimes by envy of the Dutch success. They also need to be considered alongside the admiration which many Englishmen felt for the provision made for poor relief.

Hostile English pamphleteers often found it possible to combine criticisms of Dutch financiers and merchants with derisive remarks about the Dutch as 'butter-boxes' and 'cheese-mongers'. This serves

38 *The Milkmaid*, by Gerrit Bleker.

to remind us that the Dutch were farmers as well as businessmen, particularly in the eastern provinces. The cattle which are to be seen on the canvases of Cuyp and Paulus Potter were among the best in Europe, aided by the early introduction of root crops and systems of crop rotation which made it possible to keep cattle alive through the winter. Dairy produce was plentiful, though the peasants themselves seem to have taken their butter to market and eaten their cheese on unbuttered bread. The existence of large city populations encouraged intensive tillage and also the growth of market gardening; it is possible that more vegetables were eaten in the Netherlands than anywhere else in Europe. There was also some specialization in industrial crops – flax for linen, dyes for the cloth industry, barley and hops for brewing. Enterprise and experiment were to be seen here too. The convivial peasants painted by Jan Steen, Brouwer and Ostade had little enough to celebrate, but, cushioned as they were against the disaster of a bad harvest by the importation of grain from the Baltic, they were better off than their fellows in most of France, and few of them felt the urge to emigrate in search of land across the sea.

Butter-boxes and cheese-mongers though some of the Dutch may have been, most of them were, in the phrase which Napoleon later applied to the English, 'a nation of shopkeepers', and they were a nation of city dwellers. The Netherlands had long been one of the most highly urbanized areas in Europe, and in the seventeenth century a majority of the population of the largest province in the Dutch Republic, that of Holland itself, lived in towns. By twentieth-century standards the density of population was not great, and the towns were not large. When the Revolt began only Amsterdam had as many as 30,000 inhabitants. By about 1620 Haarlem and Leiden may have had 40,000 inhabitants, Rotterdam some 20,000 and others were smaller; Amsterdam had become one of the dozen or so European cities with more than 100,000 people.

By 1700 Amsterdam had roughly doubled this figure, including within its boundaries about 10 per cent of the population of the Dutch Republic, and was becoming more like a modern city in size; but it was still far inferior to London just across the North Sea. Rotterdam too had grown to 80,000. What was important, however, was less the precise size of the towns than the fact that such a high proportion of the population lived within these civic communities, all those in Holland being within an area some 60 miles square. The far-flung interests which extended to every corner of the globe were rooted in intense local loyalties – much of Dutch history can be seen as a tension between cosmopolitan and local interests – and the richest and most powerful people in Dutch society were members of urban patriciates, not landed proprietors.

A landed nobility did exist, particularly in some of the eastern provinces such as Gelderland, but its estates were not large enough to give the social prestige and power enjoyed by other aristocracies. Titles without large estates were of little account, particularly as there was no monarch to make new creations and stimulate rivalries. Many nobles found careers in the army, and therefore looked to the princes of Orange, who held the position of Captain-General, and became keen Orangists; others were not easily distinguishable from the great families in the towns. There was little incentive for merchants who had made their pile to seek to buy a social position by acquiring a country estate, as in England – and there were certainly many more profitable investments. The practice did develop of purchasing a

39 Naïve but realistic sketch of a street in Leiden in about 1650.

40 Below left, Dutch housewives make their purchases in the market at Rotterdam: *The Great Market at Rotterdam*, by Hendrik Sorgh.

41 *The Market Place and Grote Kerk at Haarlem*, painting by Gerrit Berckheyde (below).

manor and calling oneself *Heer van* . . .; but even this was more in the second half of the seventeenth century than the first, and in any case those who did so did not forget that their position and power came from their membership of the city oligarchies.

Oligarchies they certainly were, both before and after the Revolt, for the burghers had long since lost any rights that they had once possessed in the election of their *vroedschap*, or city council. Only in times of crisis might the members of the ornamental civic militia known as the *schutterij* (themselves well-to-do, for they had to provide their equipment and their functions were largely social) seek to play a part in civic affairs – as in Amsterdam in 1578, when in the *coup* known as the *Alteratie*, the old pro-Spanish and Roman Catholic ruling clique was turned out, and the *schutterij* proceeded to choose a new Council. Three years later the States sanctioned the new patriciate, but forbade city governments for the future to seek the advice of the guilds and the *schutterij*: the *Alteratie* was not to be a precedent.

Members of the Council held their positions for life and vacancies were filled by co-option. At Amsterdam there were thirty-six of them; they met annually to make nominations for the seven *schepenen*, or aldermen; former *schepenen* and burgomasters met annually to choose from among their own number three people to act as burgomasters for the ensuing year; and these three chose one of the retiring burgomasters to make up their number to four. Thus the burgomasters were chosen from a restricted circle and might be frequently re-elected. They were the real rulers of the city, free from much effective control by the council. Directly or indirectly they made most appointments to the many minor civic offices, and their influence in the choice of the *schepenen* was usually decisive; they preserved order, approved sentences of death and banishment, regulated guilds, kept a vigilant eye on the church and dominated city policy on national issues. The main features of these arrangements are found in the other Dutch cities as well, though numbers and details varied, and often burgomasters were elected directly by the *vroedschap*. There was no pretence at uniformity in the Republic, and no two cities were identical.

Authority in the cities was therefore in the hands of a few people drawn from a small group of 'regent' or ruling families. (The Dutch word 'regent', which we shall adopt, implies no suggestion of deputizing for someone else.) These families were often closely knit by

42 The magistrates of Deventer, as painted by Gerard ter Borch in 1667: the group portrait was hung in the Town Hall at Deventer.

intermarriage. Of seventeen Amsterdam burgomasters between 1578 and 1590, there were nine whose sons or sons-in-law later filled the office, and this tendency grew with time. In the early seventeenth century, however, it was still possible for self-made men from outside to break into the circle, particularly with the aid of a well-chosen marriage. Jacob Poppen, who died as burgomaster in 1624, leaving a fortune not far short of a million florins, was the son of a man who began his career as a poor clerk in an Amsterdam office, married his master's daughter and was one of the founders of the East India Company. The great family of the Witsens dated from two brothers who came to Amsterdam from the village of Akersloot: one was employed in herring-packing, the other in shipping, working first for others and then on their own account; both became rich men, and one was burgomaster in 1609.

43 *The Company of
Frans Banningh Cocq*, commonly
known as *The Night Watch*.
Part of the Civic Guard during
Marie de Medici's visit to
Amsterdam in 1638, the company
is commemorated by Rembrandt
in a work intended to be hung
in the Hall of the Civic Guard.

Frans Banningh Cocq, immortalized by his inclusion in the so-called *Night Watch*, was the son of a man born in Bremen, who was said to have begged on the streets when he first came to Amsterdam, but who married into an Amsterdam family dating back to the fourteenth century and eventually moved into a house on the Herengracht. Frans was a member of the *vroedschap* at twenty-nine, and eventually four times burgomaster, aided by the fact that he was the brother-in-law of Cornelis de Graeff. Another subject of Rembrandt's brush, Dr Nicolaes Tulp, was the son of a linen-merchant. Acquiring a considerable fortune from his practice as a physician – he is said to have been the first to visit his patients in a carriage, from his new house on the Keizersgracht – he must also have been one of the first members of the medical profession to become the burgomaster of a great city. It has been remarked that, if we know Tulp through Rembrandt, their contemporaries first knew Rembrandt through Tulp. As for the Trips, for whom Rembrandt painted four portraits, they came from humble beginnings in Zaltbommel, arrived in Amsterdam by way of Dordrecht, and, though Elias Trip was also active in the East India Company, built up vast wealth principally by dealings in munitions of every kind; they supplied both Roundheads and Cavaliers with arms, and were alternately in partnership and

44, 45 The generations contrasted: Andries Bicker, the austere father, and Gerard Bicker, the dissipated son.

46, 47 Father and son:
Nicolaes Tulp, the physician,
here portrayed by Frans Hals,
and Diedrick Tulp,
by Paulus Potter.

rivalry with the great de Geer who exploited the iron, copper and armaments industries of Sweden. Elias's nephew was the first to become alderman and burgomaster, and the family was soon related by marriage not only to de Geer but also to the great Amsterdam families of Bicker and de Graeff.

Thus it was possible to get taken into the class of regents by a combination of supreme business skill and appropriate marriages; yet it became increasingly harder to do this as the decades passed. Characteristic of the middle years of the seventeenth century were the figures of Cornelis de Graeff (of whom it was said that he could have given Aristotle a lesson in politics) and the brothers Bicker – Jacob, who brought corn from the Baltic, Andries, who imported furs from Russia, Cornelis, whose interests were mainly in the West Indies and South America, and Jan, who traded with the Mediterranean and the Levant. Their families were at the core of the

Amsterdam patriciate; they were of course related by marriage, and Jan de Witt's wife was the niece alike of Cornelis de Graeff and of the brothers Bicker. Their influence in the politics of the city was far greater than that of any of the others just mentioned.

Until the middle of the seventeenth century the regents were themselves intimately concerned with trade. The flag of the Bickers seemed to the poet Vondel to be ubiquitous, and was sufficiently so to arouse the jealousy of some of the other regents. But at about the same time complaints began to occur that some of them had ceased to trade, and had become *rentiers* investing in the funds and in property. Some, like Jan de Witt's father, had their sons educated for

48 Rembrandt's portrait of Margaretha de Geer, wife of Jacob Trip.

49 The Trippenhuis, built by Philips Vingboons.

lives of public service rather than commercial activity; some encouraged their sons to travel abroad on a kind of 'grand tour' like the English gentry. They had the wealth and the assured social position to enable them to do this. 'Such', wrote Sir William Temple, 'were most or all of the chief ministers ... not men of mean or mechanic trades as it is commonly received among foreigners, and makes the subject of comical jests upon their government.'

Dutch preachers and pamphleteers also began to criticize a decline in the frugality and sobriety which had been characteristic of their regents at the beginning of the seventeenth century; and the new houses, like those which went up on the Amsterdam *grachten*, or the classical Trippenhuis which was built for the brothers Trip in 1662 (now the Royal Academy of Sciences), were certainly more expensive than the old. The gaudy and dissipated look of Gerard Bicker contrasts sharply with the black-and-white portrait of his father Andries; while the sober Nicolaes Tulp's son, Diedrick (who received a baronetcy from Charles II of England) seems in a different world from his father in the equestrian portrait by Paulus Potter which occupies the whole of one wall in the house of Jan Six, the prominent art collector.

Yet to a foreign observer like Temple, accustomed to the luxurious living of English aristocrats and courtiers, the moderation and unpretentiousness of the regents still seemed remarkable in 1672. For him, the greatness of the Dutch state consisted especially in 'the good choice of the offices of chief trust in the cities, provinces, and state: and the great simplicity and modesty in the common port or living of their chiefest ministers; without which, the absoluteness of the Senates in each town, and the immensity of taxes throughout the whole state, would never be endured by the people with any patience; being both of them greater than in many of those governments, which are esteemed most arbitrary among their neighbours.'

A tendency to increasing luxury, and to a divorce between business and the magistracy, might be ominous for the future; but for a long time a relative community of interest and moderation in the style of living minimized any risk of conflict between the regents and the ordinary burghers. The salary of the burgomasters of Amsterdam, Temple commented, was a mere 500 guilders, or £50, per annum. No doubt there were other perquisites to be obtained, but it is abundantly clear that the main incentive in seeking office lay in the status, power and patronage which it gave, rather than as a source of wealth. Temple, who as English ambassador had good opportunities to know, thought highly of the public spirit of the burgomasters when he wrote in 1672; some of the implied comparisons with the England of Charles II are not flattering.

It is likely that Temple's remarks are to some extent idealized. Generalizations about classes like the regents are difficult to make. Judgments cannot, in the nature of things, be much more than subjective impressions. Both in the history of Amsterdam and in that of lesser cities it is not difficult to find examples of self-seeking (as when the burgomasters profited from the plans to extend Amsterdam in 1612), favouritism towards relatives, intrigue, factions and parochialism in outlook. Yet when these inevitable reservations have been made, some may well think that in honesty, ability and sense of public responsibility the regents compare well with the royal favourites, aristocratic magnates and their clients in other countries.

Why was the remainder of the urban populations content to accept exclusion from civic affairs by this comparatively small minority? There were plenty of other people with the necessary education and political knowledge, yet demands for participation were few. But Dutch society generally was characterized by a devotion to traditional rights, privileges and methods of doing things, and people were prepared to accept the rule of the 'natural rulers of society'. Moreover, their rule was on the whole successful, providing the conditions for growing prosperity, at least for the articulate citizens and, to a certain extent, even for the lowest classes, particularly when the relatively generous provision for poor relief is taken into account. The regents, continuing to live in their city houses, were in touch with the interests and sentiments of their citizens and took care not to outrage them. Again, public office in the larger cities like Amsterdam was very time-consuming, and others preferred to get on with their business concerns. Finally, the city councils were large enough not to be altogether homogeneous (at least for the greater part of the seventeenth century) so that minority views could find expression, and 'the Establishment' did not seem entirely closed.

On the whole, therefore, the authority of the city oligarchies was uncontested. Occasionally, however, there was violent protest. The members of the civic militias so often painted by Dutch artists no longer had any worth-while military functions to perform, and they existed almost entirely for the sake of enormous occasional banquets – the magistrates of Haarlem in 1621 laid down that they were not to last longer than three, or at the most four, days. But once or twice, particularly when they could be used to support one faction on the Council, they had some political importance, as in the *Alteratie* already mentioned, and more widely in the great crisis year of 1672. They had their property to consider, however, and often one or two members of regent families acted as officers, so they were not likely to engage in any really revolutionary action. Lower down was the dreaded *grauw*, the rabble, although it is now coming to be recognized that the *grauw*, like other 'mobs' in history, included not merely 'the

50 Frans Hals, *Banquet of the Officers of the Militia Company of St George*, 1616.

dregs of the population' but small shopkeepers, artisans and respectable people, regarded as 'rabble' only by the people at the top. Two things could bring them out onto the streets. A new and oppressive addition to the numbers of indirect taxes could occasionally lead to a riot; and sometimes Calvinist preachers, particularly in a time of depression or national defeat, could whip up passions. In neither case did the disorders merge into effective demands for a radical reconstruction of government.

As for the inhabitants of the villages, they fell under the influence of nobles (in provinces like Gelderland), or of townspeople who bought land in the countryside (as in Holland); or, like the freeholders of Friesland and Groningen, they enjoyed a certain amount of independence. But whatever their importance to Dutch agriculture, and exclusive as the local village community often became, they could be ignored on the larger political scene.

POLITICAL INSTITUTIONS

In the province of Holland there were eighteen towns which possessed the traditional right to send delegations to the body known as the States of Holland, meeting, usually four times a year, for some weeks, in the Binnenhof at The Hague. Each delegation could be as large as the town wished, but the town had only one vote. Once, no doubt, the towns had been much closer to one another in size, but by 1600 the disparity between Amsterdam, at one extreme, and a small decayed town like Purmerend, at the other, had become vast. Yet there was no thought of depriving the 'rotten boroughs' of votes, or of giving the vote to expanding communities like The Hague, 'the largest village in Europe', or the thronging population of the ship-building areas on the Zaanstreek. The nobility of the province also sent a delegation which, like each town, gave a block vote. The fact that the single vote of the nobility was pronounced first sometimes gave it a little more weight, but it remained one vote, in comparison with eighteen from the towns.

On important matters, however, it was rare for the votes of a majority to overrule the protests of an important minority. It was in any case impossible for the States to employ coercion on a recalcitrant town, particularly if that town were Amsterdam, which paid about a quarter of the taxation of the entire Republic. In cases of serious disagreement, the delegations might report the situation back to their principals at home and ask for further instructions, or they might respond to manipulation by the permanent official known in the early days of the Republic as the Advocate and later as the Pensionary; he might suggest a compromise, or urge the minority to withdraw so that a consensus might be achieved. This often meant that important decisions could not be reached quickly, and that a great deal depended on the skill, patience and political connections of the Pensionary.

Originally the Pensionary of the province (the cities each had their own) was only a legal adviser and spokesman, but the office was greatly developed by the personality of its holders, who were able to make use of the advantages which a permanent official always has over changing members of delegations. Technically, after Oldenbarnevelt's time, tenure of office was for five years, but it was almost invariably renewed. Into the Pensionary's hands fell the task of preparing and carrying out decisions, formulating resolutions, providing information and carrying on correspondence. Almost inevitably he became in practice the nearest thing to a minister of state, not only in the province of Holland, but, since this was by far the most important of the provinces, in the Republic as a whole. It should be stressed that none of the most prominent holders of the office came from Amsterdam. Oldenbarnevelt, who was Advocate from 1586 to 1618, came from Rotterdam; de Witt, who was Pensionary from 1653 to 1672, came from Dordrecht; Fagel (1672–88) from Haarlem; and Heinsius (1689–1720) from Delft. Leading Amsterdammers preferred to wield power in their own city, and often were reluctant even to risk losing it by becoming a member of a delegation at The Hague. This increased the tendency for Amsterdam, by virtue of its size and wealth, to enjoy a semi-independent status within the province and within the Republic.

The province of Holland was the richest and most populous; it included all the largest cities and contributed some 58 per cent of the Union's budget. Yet it was only one of seven provinces which were theoretically equal in status. Each of the provinces had its own assembly of States, and all these bodies were constituted differently. The details would be tedious to recount, and the briefest description must suffice. In the other trading province of Zeeland, the States, meeting in the great abbey at Middelburg, consisted of the First Noble (who, by virtue of his lordship of Vlissingen and marquisate of Veere, was the Prince of Orange or his representative) and delegations

51 The Knights' Hall in the Binnenhof, The Hague: painting by an anonymous contemporary.

from Middelburg and five other towns. The Prince of Orange thus had a stronger power base here than in Holland. In some of the landward provinces, too, his influence, though informal, was great, because society was more agrarian, and the nobility was relatively more numerous, and tended to look to the Princes for promotion in the army and for other favours. In Gelderland, for instance, the representation of nobles and towns was technically equal, but in practice nobles often had town houses and even sat on the councils. In Overijssel the proportions were equal between the nobility and the three cities of Deventer, Kampen and Zwolle. In Utrecht the balance in practice was much the same, though the details were complicated by survivals from the city's episcopal past. In the far north-east, in Groningen, one vote belonged to the city magistrates and the other to the representatives of 144 parishes, based on a landed qualification; these latter were in effect the local squirearchy, but some of the citizens had purchased land. Finally, in Friesland, the cities possessed one vote and the countryside three; the franchise in the country belonged to the freeholders, who were numerous, but the elections were (in the words of a modern authority) 'at best public entertainment, at worst public scandals'.

Each of the seven provinces was complete master in its own house, and each sent a delegation to the assembly of the States-General. In the eyes of the outside world this was the governing body in the Republic, but in fact it was a meeting of allies rather than a parliamentary assembly, and important decisions were supposed to require the agreement of all the provinces, not a majority vote of the delegations present. The Union of Utrecht of 1579 had been in effect a temporary defensive alliance among the provinces to meet the immediate demands of the struggle against Spain; those concerned in it had not attempted to frame a constitution with unified central institutions and a common executive. The prosecution and financing of the war was the primary concern, and the States-General existed for this purpose, to discuss consequent problems of foreign relations and to perform certain functions such as the granting of charters to the East and West India Companies; but it did not, at least after Leicester's departure, legislate on domestic matters.

At first the States-General was thought of as an extraordinary body, but from 1593 it met daily, usually between 11 and 1, Sundays not excepted, and, after some variation in earlier years, it came to sit in the Binnenhof, near to the States of Holland and the quarters of the Pensionary. It was not inevitable that it should become fixed here; it might seem that the principal city, Amsterdam, would be an appropriate place, but Amsterdam was one of the latest cities to joint the Revolt and was regarded jealously by many others, so that the old seat of the Counts of Holland at The Hague ('s Gravenhage) was adopted, with important consequences for Dutch political history. There its members met, received foreign ambassadors, and became the 'Hogen-Mogen men', the High and Mighty States-General of the official documents.

Each province could send as many delegates as it wished. The small size of the room limited the number that could attend at any one time, but delegates could easily alternate. Usually there would be about thirty persons sitting round the table, with the provinces taking turns, week by week, to provide a president. The Pensionary of Holland always attended with the Holland delegation, and the same factors

52 The office of the Admiralty at Amsterdam, most powerful of the five Admiralties.

which operated in the long service of Oldenbarnevelt to give him an ascendancy in the States of Holland did so in the States-General too, even though the Pensionary was not formally a 'minister' of the Union. His influence was that of the well-informed, able, long-surviving effective leader of one provincial delegation, whose knowledge and experience enabled him to cajole and manipulate his colleagues – it was not the result of authority belonging to any office that he held. If agreement was to be reached, he was indispensable. Yet he had to proceed carefully, for though his own province was the largest and richest, the others for this very reason were jealous of their rights, and could never be coerced into agreement. Often the interests of the landward provinces did not coincide with those of the trading provinces of Holland and Zeeland, and decisions on matters of war and peace might take a long time. Frequently discussions had to be adjourned while delegations returned home to consult their provincial States, or the committees which sat during the intervals between their sessions, and foreign ambassadors were exasperated by the delays inseparable from all negotiations. It was this which made Temple's success in concluding the Triple Alliance of 1668 in five days so remarkable; but that was only possible because de Witt was able to exercise remarkable powers of persuasion on his colleagues.

Apart from a Council of State, which after the early years was of only minor importance, and a *rekenkamer* to control expenditure, the States-General was virtually the only institution which was common to all the provinces. One of the articles of the Union of Utrecht had foreshadowed a common tax for purposes of defence, but, as William the Silent had foreseen, no such system came into existence, apart from the *convooien en licenten* raised by the Admiralty Colleges on imports and exports, and a stamp duty. Instead, the annual revenue required for the purposes of the Republic was divided into quotas for each province. The means of raising the quota was left to the province concerned; and if, as sometimes happened, a province failed to raise the full amount, there was no way of coercing it, and indeed no supervision over the provinces' finances. One result was that regiments came to be divided among the provinces for purposes of pay, and, since he who paid the piper inevitably wished to call the tune, the provinces influenced appointments, and even expected officers to take an oath to them, as well as to the States-General and the Captain-General.

The provincial taxes themselves showed local variations, inequalities and abuses; most important were the taxes on consumption, which were levied on a wide variety of commodities and entrusted not to an official bureaucracy but to tax-farmers, who were violently unpopular, even occasionally to the point of rioting. The States-General several times tried to reduce the confused currency situation to order; but there were mints in each province. If there was no uniform system of taxation in the Republic, there was no uniform legal system either; there were no central courts, and nothing was done to codify the varying local and provincial customs. Even the date varied from province to province. Holland and Zeeland had adopted the New Style in 1582; the other provinces did not do so until 1700; and servants of the States-General often found it convenient to employ both, Old and New.

One might have expected that when circumstances made it necessary to set up new institutions, this would have been done on a national basis. On the contrary, every concession was made to local interests. In 1597 the States-General decided to make provision for naval administration, the collection of the import and export duties, matters relating to prizes, and so on. For these purposes, it set up not one Admiralty, but five: one for the area of the Maas, based at Rotterdam, and first in rank; one at Amsterdam, the most powerful; one in the North Quarter, alternating between Hoorn and Enkhuizen; one in Zeeland, at Middelburg; and one in Friesland. There was frequent discussion of the need to set up a general supervisory commission, but nothing was done; and the result was that co-operation was extremely sketchy, and the various sections of the fleet were never ready at the same time. Various precedences and privileges soon grew up; for instance, de Ruyter's biographer tells us that he was 'granted the privilege of continuing to live at Amsterdam and work under the Admiralty of that town, although the Rotterdam Admiralty came in rank before that of Amsterdam. The old custom, according to which the Lieutenant-Admiral always sailed from Rotterdam, and used a ship of the Maas Admiralty as flagship, would, however, continue to be observed. Amsterdam . . . tried to obtain a reversal of this decision, but was unsuccessful, and in this respect at least Rotterdam preserved its ancient privileges.' In war-time the task of fitting out the fleet every spring must have been extraordinarily complicated by the necessity to observe customary niceties.

The charters of the East and West India Companies, though these were intended to be trading companies and not political institutions, illustrate the same need to propitiate local jealousies. The price for the combination of the different groups which had first tried to exploit the new East India trade into one monopolistic company was the establishment in 1602 of a kind of federation of six chambers, each of which, it was intended, should possess a measure of trading autonomy within the main lines of policy laid down by the directors, the 'Heren XVII'. These, it was specified, should consist of eight from Amsterdam, four from Zeeland, one each from the chambers of Hoorn, Enkhuizen, Rotterdam and Delft, and one other elected either from Zeeland or one of the smaller chambers; they were to meet for six years in Amsterdam, and two in Middelburg. Each local chamber had its own employees, and its own ships and crew which must return to their own port; and it can easily be imagined that in the local chambers vacancies were effectively filled by the city magistrates, and those appointed held office for life. As time went on Amsterdam's share was increased in practice, because Amsterdam merchants participated in the other chambers; and a sort of permanent secretariat came into existence at The Hague under Pieter van Dam. But in the meantime local pride was satisfied, and local interests and central direction were reconciled. When the West India Company was established twenty years later, its organization was similar, except that its directors were the 'Heren XIX', and included one official representative of the States-General.

To the modern reader the political arrangement of the Dutch Republic will seem haphazard and cumbersome, undemocratic, and in danger of giving too much weight to parochial interests at the expense of a common national policy.

It was certainly not the most efficient of constitutions. Although in many other respects the Dutch found imitators, there was never any possibility that anyone would wish to copy their political institutions. The need to refer back from States-General to the provinces, and from provinces to towns, and back again, in what could be a very slow process of consultation, meant that no quick decisions, and no sharp changes of policy could be undertaken. The wheels were often clogged by routine. Secrecy was almost out of the question; it was notorious that foreign diplomats found it easier here than anywhere else to find out what was going on, and even to obtain, for a price, copies of official secret documents. Yet somehow agreement was reached, sometimes after an appropriate amount of manipulation and straining of the law, and practical solutions were found.

The English are sometimes accused of having a genius for 'muddling through', but this could easily be applied also to the Dutch in the seventeenth century. They had long sat together to concert action, not only on town councils but on many other bodies too. Far back into the Middle Ages there had existed a medley of authorities to look after dykes, drainage and local waterways; it has been said that about 500 of the boards still existing in 1952 dated back to medieval times, and that in older times it was not uncommon to find some twenty *waterschap* officials in villages of fifty or sixty householders. In this vital respect, in the government of villages and of towns, there was a long tradition of discussion and somehow working out what needed to be done, and so it was in state politics too. The Revolt against Spain itself had taken place to defend local 'liberties' and traditions, not to call for a radical political reconstruction, whether based on theories of utility or of natural rights. As long as the Republic was moving successfully forward, the machinery might creak, but it did not often cause serious dissatisfaction. In 1651 the States-General called a special Great Assembly to discuss what changes were needed, but it dispersed without making far-reaching alterations. It was much later, in the eighteenth century, that the system proved incapable of adaptation to make new policies when they were required.

Dutch society has been referred to as a 'bourgeois democracy', but the term democracy is only apposite if it is used in contrast to a society based on a landed aristocracy or a monarchical court. It has no application if it is intended to imply that any of its political institutions was based on participation by popular election. The States-General, provincial Estates and town councils were dominated by the regent class, and a minority of nobles. Some parts of the Dutch Republic were not represented in the States-General, even in the most indirect way. In the north-east, Drenthe paid a financial contribution in return for military protection and internal autonomy, but it had no share in any policy discussions in the States-General. More serious was the fate of the so-called 'Generality Lands' in northern Brabant and elsewhere, taken from Spain by Frederick Henry, younger brother of Prince Maurice, between 1629 and 1637. These were treated essentially as conquered territories over which the States-General exercised direct and irresponsible authority. Brabant several times petitioned for representation, only to be refused, partly because the area was overwhelmingly Catholic, and partly because it was thought that in practice the princes of Orange would be able to appoint any delegation and use it for their own purposes. But even in those seven provinces that were represented, the delegations were not the result of any democratic process, and they were drawn from the exclusive patrician class.

It is easy, therefore, to describe the United Provinces as being a narrow oligarchy. Yet its narrowness can be exaggerated. Often a real public opinion existed which could not be ignored. The populations of the towns of Holland were probably the most literate and the best informed, on both Dutch and international matters, in Europe. They had to be, in the interests of trade, which could be disturbed by any war or internal commotion. Merchants who had relatives or factors in foreign lands – and there were 'colonies' of Dutchmen in all the great European seaports – were expected to supply information about other things than prices. A much wider circle was reached by the printed newsletters, the *corantos*, which were a feature of the Republic. It was for a long time the only country where private persons could publish news under licence. The earliest known Dutch *coranto* dates from 1618, but the newsletters soon proliferated, no doubt under the stimulus of a demand for news in the early years of the Thirty Years' War. They were based on the systematic collection of reports from all over Europe, and even had arrangements for alterations to accommodate 'stop press' news.

In addition, a mass of controversial pamphlet literature poured out from Dutch presses. Knuttel's catalogue of pamphlets preserved in the Royal Library runs into five figures for the years between 1579 and

A *coranto* of 1633, with reports
m Rome and Venice.

54 *The Pamphlet Seller*, by Jan van der Vliet: an engraving of 1630.

Alsoomen over eenighe daghen doende was in 't Casteel van Sint Angel om eenighe Fonda= menten te verstercken / isser in 't graven ghevonden een kopere Coffer vol ghemunt ghelt over tcklijcke hondert Jaren gheslaghen ten tij= e van Alaricus ende andere Gottische Co= nghen boorsaten der Sweeden. Hier over n de gheesten der vernuftighe Rijmers won= er besigh om eenighe uptlegginghe hier over te oen.

Den Hertogh van Merceur ende den Prince an Martignes zijn huyden morghen van Na= les hier weder aenghecomen / zijnde seer heer= ch inghehaelt. Sy hebben hun afschept ghe= omen van den Paus / ende keeren weder uaer ranckrijck.

Wt Venetien den 18 May.

Den Hertogh van Parma heeft groote achten gedaen aenden Gouverneur van Mi= anen / over 'tghewelt vande Spaensche Sol= aten / die ettelijcke Dorpen onder Parma oorende / gheleghen aende Frontieren van dilanen uptgheplondert ende heel afghebrant ebben. Maer den Spaenschen Gouverneur doof aen dat oor. Het is oock waer ende se= er dat hy na alle Edellieden van Milanen aen aren Gouverneur ghepresenteert hebben over ghegeven ende transporteren alle hun incom= en / midts conditie dat hy dan zijne Soldaten aer mede selfs soude onderhouden / sonder m langher daer mede te beswaren. Versoec= ende publique Acte van dese hare presentatie.

1713. They did not have to be submitted for censorship, as in England under the terms of the Star Chamber ordinance of 1586, or the Licensing Act of 1662; and although afterwards foreign ambassadors might occasionally complain of something offensive that had been published, it very seldom resulted in any serious inconvenience to the author, who could in any case slip away from the jurisdiction of one set of magistrates to another city. Some of the polemics were reasoned, others abusive; but they are so voluminous as to make it impossible to believe that the regents, living in their city houses, were totally indifferent either to their arguments or to their irrational prejudices. They were not so exclusive as to be able to cut themselves off from public opinion, and to that extent the Dutch system was more 'democratic' than others.

Of course the governments of most European states in the seventeenth century gave far more scope to local variations than would be generally thought desirable today. The external frontiers of the most 'absolute' of them, like France, though neat and tidy on the map, concealed within them internal customs barriers, and a variety of legal jurisdictions, local franchises and institutions which persisted down to the late eighteenth century. Provinces which had been annexed to the main body, whether by succession or by conquest, over centuries, tended to be allowed to preserve their idiosyncratic customs and privileges unless there were very good reasons for interfering with them; rational criticism and modification came later. Yet the constitution of the United Provinces gave more scope to local liberties, at the expense of central direction, than was the case elsewhere. Central institutions were fewer and weaker, there was less of a paid state bureaucracy, and more opportunity for the rulers of cities like Amsterdam to hinder the development of a consistent state policy in their own local interests. As will be seen, the looseness of the Dutch system (if indeed it can be called a system) had its advantages; but there was a case for believing that the muddle, the apparent inefficiencies, the self-interest of the regents and the exaltation of local particularism at the expense of national interests needed to be controlled by the guiding hand of a princely ruler. Those who thought in this way – and the sixteenth and seventeenth centuries were a period in which most men thought in terms of princes and courts – along with others whose motives were those of self-advancement, turned instinctively towards the House of Orange.

55 William I of Orange, assassinated in 1584, united the Dutch under his leadership in the revolt against Spain.

THE PRINCES OF ORANGE

In the early days of the Union many people had thought that the rebel cause could not survive unless the Dutch found a prince to lead them. Offering the sovereignty to a foreigner, rather than a Netherlands noble, had the double advantage that, if the offer were accepted, an ally would be brought into the struggle against Spain, while the mutual jealousies of native families would be avoided. Accordingly sovereignty was offered alternately to the King of France's brother, the Duke of Anjou, and to Queen Elizabeth herself. Neither idea turned out well. The Duke of Anjou, frustrated to find his freedom of action very severely restricted by the States-General and the towns of Holland, attempted a *coup* in 1583 against Antwerp (then still in rebel hands) and failed ignominiously. The Earl of Leicester, at the head of 5,000 English troops, accepted the title of Governor-General in 1586 contrary to Elizabeth's orders, quarrelled with the regents of Holland, allied himself with a popular party in Utrecht, achieved no military success – indeed his officers betrayed two towns to the Spaniards – and departed in similar disrepute in 1587. The two episodes served to convince the States-General not to put their trust in foreign princes, and to make them resolve to rely on their own efforts.

The House of Orange, however, was intimately bound up with the struggle against Spain in its darkest days. William the Silent enjoyed a reputation to which neither Anjou nor Leicester could aspire. He was not the kind of military hero who often leads movements for national independence; trust in him was founded on his unquestioned patriotism, his ability to inspire confidence in the hour of need, and his patient skill in inducing local politicians to sink their jealousies in the co-operative effort. The bullets which struck him down in the Prinsenhof at Delft in 1584 removed Philip II's greatest enemy, but established him permanently in the popular memory as the Father of his country, who had given up his life for it. It was natural that his descendants should aspire to the offices he had held, and natural that many should be favourably disposed to their claims.

The offices in question were those of stadholder and Captain-General. The word 'stadholder' is the literal equivalent of 'lieutenant'; each of the seven provinces in the Union had such an officer, theoretically taking the place of the ruler and responsible for public order and the administration of justice (though the latter duty amounted to little but a modified right of pardon). When Habsburg rule had been thrown off, it fell to the provincial States to make the appointment. At no time during our period was the same member of the House of Orange stadholder of all the seven provinces; it was usual for a cousin to hold the office in the northern provinces of Friesland and Groningen, while the most important member of the family was stadholder in the rest, with something like a princely court at The Hague. The duties of the stadholder were ill-defined, save that in the Union of Utrecht it was agreed that he should have some general competence to compose quarrels among the members of the Union. Sometimes theory and practice were at variance; the stadholder was supposed to have the right to choose some city magistrates from a short list presented to him, but except in certain crises this must have been a formality. In other ways his influence was greater than it appeared to be; for instance, he did not preside over the deliberations of the States-General and when he appeared there he had only an advisory voice, but behind the scenes he had ways of influencing the composition and the policies of the delegations of some of the landward provinces, like Gelderland.

In any case the Prince of Orange was a prince, and this always gave him a certain prestige, even in a republic; this helps to explain why, for instance, William III was so resentful of the occupation of the

56 The Nassau 'Cavalcade': prominent members of the House of Orange on parade. Leading the group, first and second from the right, are Prince Maurice and Prince Frederick Henry.

principality of Orange (in the south of France) by Louis XIV. The prince was not merely a noble like others, or even a stadholder; he was the centre of a real Court, French-speaking, sophisticated and extravagant, even though in scale, expense and elaboration of etiquette it was not the equal of the courts of the Habsburgs and Bourbons. It was natural for foreign ambassadors, though officially accredited to the States-General, to discuss matters with him. Moreover, as Captain-General, the Prince led the army and usually had the greatest say in the appointment of its higher officers, and this was an added reason why ambitious soldiers of noble birth should attach themselves to him. He was Admiral-General, too, but only in 1688 did he command a fleet in person, and though his influence in the navy was not negligible, it fell short of his authority in the army.

As Prince, Captain-General of the armed forces of the Republic, stadholder of more than one province, and traditional leader in the war of independence, the head of the House of Orange occupied a special position in the Union. He was not the servant of only one province, as was the Pensionary of Holland; he could be a unifying force, bringing together the disparate local elements into one common effort, and foreseeing the general need as William the Silent had done. On the other hand, by virtue of his position as Captain-General his authority would be much greater in time of war than in peace – as would his income; when the Treaty of Münster, which put an end to the 'Eighty Years' War', was being negotiated in 1647, William II estimated that it would mean the loss of two-thirds of his revenue. If the princes were uniquely placed to give leadership in war, they also had a vested interest in it.

The pressures towards monarchy were so great in most of Europe that it is natural to wonder why the princes of Orange did not establish themselves as a dynasty until the kingdom of the Netherlands was set up in 1814. To a certain extent this was the result of a run of bad luck. William the Silent was on the point of being made Count of Holland when his life was cut short in 1584. His eldest son Philip William had been brought up a Catholic in Spain; he had not been seen in the Netherlands for many years and never had any chance of being accepted there. His second son, Maurice of Nassau, was a boy of seventeen when his father was killed. At Oldenbarnevelt's prompting Maurice was rapidly made the stadholder of five provinces, partly as a counterpoise to Leicester; he became a great military leader with a special expertise in new and scientific methods of warfare, and showed both skill and lack of scruple in gradually working his way into a strong political position. But he succeeded as Prince of Orange only in 1618, and by the time he had overthrown Oldenbarnevelt in the crisis of that year and reached a position of dominance in the Republic, he was getting on in years, lethargic, and without the legitimate son

57 Coat of arms of Prince Maurice, encircled by the Order of the Garter.

58 Prince Maurice visits the horsefair at Valkenburg: detail from the painting by Adriaen van de Vanne.

59, 60 Bronze plaques from 1626 showing Prince Frederick Henry and Amalia von Solms, his wife.

61 Prince Frederick Henry and Amalia von Solms: portrait by Gerrit Honthorst.

who would have provided an incentive to exploit his success. Before he died in 1625 he did persuade his younger brother Frederick Henry to marry in order to continue the family line. Frederick Henry was remarkably successful, and his court began to look more like a royal one when it was joined first by the exiled King and Queen of Bohemia, and then by a Stuart daughter-in-law, Princess Mary.

In 1647 his son William succeeded to his offices – the only occasion for two centuries on which eldest son succeeded father as stadholder in the main line of the House of Orange. But in 1650 William died suddenly of small-pox at the age of only twenty-four, and his son, eventually to be William III of England, was not born until a few days later, so that a long minority ensued, and William did not become Captain-General until 1672. At what point he realized that he

62 Prince Maurice of Nassau,
by Michiel van Miereveld.

63 Prince William II,
by Gerrit Honthorst.

64 Orange popularity: the young Prince William is toasted and fêted in Jan Steen's *The Prince's Birthday*, *c.* 1660.

would have no children is an interesting but insoluble question. What is certain is that when Queen Mary died in 1694, there was no question of his remarrying; and the lack of children, coupled with his pre-occupations in international affairs, meant that there was no incentive to seek to change his status in the United Provinces. Before he died in 1702 he tried to ensure that his offices should pass to his cousin John Friso, who was stadholder in Friesland and Groningen; but John Friso was only a boy of 15 whose claims were easily evaded. When he was drowned in 1711 he, like William II, left only a posthumous son, and the second 'stadholderless period' lasted until 1747. This chain of family circumstances contrasts notably with the smoothness of the successions in the Hohenzollerns, another family which came to the front in the seventeenth century.

In ability the princes of Orange between William I and William III were at least equal to any other royal family of the period, whether

Stuart, Habsburg or Bourbon, and their political successes were not small; yet in a dynastic sense luck was against them. But they also contrived by their policies to arouse the opposition of many of the regents in the cities and States of the richest and largest province, Holland. The Orangists claimed that this was the result of the narrow, short-sighted and selfish outlook of the regents, pursuing their immediate commercial interests at the expense of long-term, national ones; the 'States' party complained of the ambition and authoritarianism of the princes, and of their readiness to put their personal and dynastic interests before those of the Republic. The tension which resulted was not continuous, but there were three great crises, in 1618, 1650 and 1672, each leaving wounds which took a long time to heal.

When conflict occurred, there was a tendency for the princes of Orange to line up with a majority of the provinces in the States-General against the single province of Holland (and, often, the city of Amsterdam especially), with a war-party against those who wanted peace, with the lower classes of the urban population against the regents, and with the Calvinist preachers against those who wished to keep the church tolerant and subordinate to political authority. When the situation is put in this way, it might appear that there were all the makings of civil war and social revolution. But the princes of Orange, while sometimes willing to use the threat of the *grauw* to put pressure on their opponents, took care never to allow matters to get out of hand. In the last resort they were themselves aristocrats and upholders of the existing social order. It is significant that in their hour of triumph, in 1618 and 1672, when they had the opportunity to make changes in the city magistrates, they still chose from the same regent class which had always been dominant.

The princes also had the good sense to content themselves with the reality of power instead of grasping at the shadow of titles. In 1675, the young William III, fresh from the laurels of evicting the French armies from Dutch territory, was tempted by the offer of the title of Duke of Gelderland, but refused it when he realized, from the reactions of the other provinces, that this would be an apple of discord in the Union. Others might not have been as moderate. And, so far as religion was concerned, though the princes patronized a religious party, they never committed themselves personally to it to the extent that the Stuarts did to their faiths, and they never lost touch with the views of powerful sections of their country.

65 This Calvinist cartoon shows the orthodox doctrines of Gomarus outweighing the ragbag views of his rival Arminius.

THE RELIGIOUS FOUNDATIONS

Any idea that the Revolt against Spain was the work of a unanimously Calvinist people has long since been discarded. If anything, historical thinking now errs by belittling the extent of Calvinism too much, as in a recent English work which describes the Calvinists in the 1570s as 'a tiny minority'. A minority they certainly were, but the word 'tiny' is inappropriate. The Sea Beggars of 1572 pressed themselves by force upon the cities of Holland and Zeeland, achieving their ends sometimes by methods of violence and terrorism, and sometimes by making promises (which they later broke) to the city magistrates that priests would be left unharmed and churches and monasteries unplundered. Yet they could not have imposed the Calvinist faith upon their countrymen without a bloody civil war, if the great majority of the population had been determinedly Catholic. From the beginning some of the citizens who had less property to lose than their magistrates were willing to co-operate with the Beggars; Calvinists who had fled from Alva's Council of Blood returned from exile, and, as in Amsterdam, conservative and Catholic magistrates were turned out, with a sufficient measure of popular support.

Apart from the minority who already had a positive devotion to the doctrines of Calvinism, there were many more who hated Alva's persecution of heretics, and were prepared to criticize the abuses of the pre-Reformation church, to approve the conversion of much of its wealth to secular uses, to accept the replacement of the old ritual by plain, low church services in the vernacular, and generally to move over at least to a moderate, biblical and undogmatic Protestantism. Much of this fitted in with what is commonly called the Erasmian tradition in the Netherlands, though the over-frequent use of that term probably ties it too much to one personality, however great. There were many others who wished to continue to worship in the traditional way, but, except briefly in the north-east, they had no great Catholic magnate like Guise in France to lead them, and they were in any case reluctant to co-operate with the Spanish troops who had committed such atrocities. Some did flee to the South, many remained quiet, and some aided the rebel cause.

The rebels thus had 'libertines' and some Catholics in their ranks, as well as Calvinists; but in the early years the Calvinists were naturally the most vociferous, uninhibited and committed enemies of Spain. In their case religious passion combined with the political motives which they shared with others; and, if the revolt were to collapse, whoever else might find it possible to make terms, heretics could expect no mercy from Philip II. Some had been in exile in England or Germany for their beliefs, and they were joined by others who came northwards from Flanders. Thus the Calvinists had by no means a monopoly of patriotism, but their zeal gave them an importance far greater than their numbers would suggest, and this was in effect recognized in 1573 when William announced his own conversion to Calvinism – which was certainly not the result of any extreme dogmatic belief of his own.

In Holland and Zeeland monastic property was rapidly seized and handed over to the civic authorities, and soon the church buildings themselves were taken over for Calvinist services. Images, paintings and stained glass were destroyed, and the churches adapted for a new form of worship. The congregation was grouped around a pulpit, topped by an immense wooden canopy, in a central position. Some would sit – there were special *herenbanken* provided for burgomasters and city councillors, and also for church elders and other privileged people – but most would stand to hear the Scriptures read and the Word of God preached in these newly austere surroundings. Hats were now kept on, except during prayers: they were taken off for no preacher, only for God. A visible, as well as doctrinal, transformation of the old forms of worship in all the parish churches took place quite abruptly.

The Union of Utrecht in 1579 provided for freedom of conscience for all, but in other respects its implications were more favourable to the Calvinist point of view than William of Orange himself would have liked. He preferred sufficient toleration for Catholics as well as Protestants to make it possible for all religious groups in the whole of the Netherlands to unite against the Spanish forces. In practice the preservation of the 'true Christian Reformed religion' became a foundation principle of the Union, and public Catholic worship was officially prohibited in the other provinces as well as in Holland and Zeeland.

66 Verses on the Synod of Dort, triumph of Calvinist orthodoxy, and a list of delegates present.

67 The new religious austerity; *The Interior of the Grote Kerk at Haarlem*, by Gerrit Berckheyde.

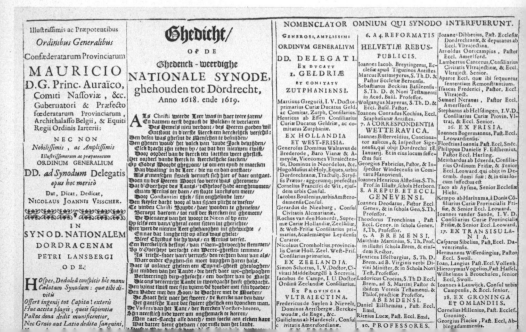

This did not mean, however, that the new Calvinist synods were allowed to have matters their own way. On the contrary, the regents were determined to ensure that there should be no danger of their being put in a position where they would have to enforce the decisions of any clerical body. They allowed no national organization to come into being. With the single exception of the famous Synod of Dort (1618), they did not permit the holding of any national synod which might aspire to the position of the Assembly of the Scottish Kirk in the seventeenth century. Permission might be given to hold provincial synods (with Holland divided into North and South for this purpose), but political commissioners were present, and the jurisdiction of the synods was limited to purely ecclesiastical matters, with exclusively ecclesiastical sanctions. No political issues could be discussed. Resolutions might be passed, calling for action against popish abuses, the activities of sects, the breaking of the Sabbath, long hair, swearing, play-acting, and the printing of dangerous books, but the provincial States did little about them; and the frequency of such resolutions suggests that many of those who voted must have realized that they would remain merely pious expressions of opinion.

In the cities, too, the councils kept a watchful eye on the consistory. All the church members living in a city were regarded as one congregation, with one consistory, and the ministers were pastors of the city, preaching in turn in the different buildings set apart for public worship, and paid from municipal funds. When there was a vacancy for the appointment of a new *predikant* in Amsterdam, the name put forward by the *kerkeraad* had to receive the approval of the burgomasters, and this was by no means a formality. There were cases when candidates were vetoed, just as there were one or two occasions when ministers who had been appointed were banished from the city for discussing political issues from the pulpit. The main concern of the regents here was not the enforcement of a particular religious policy, but the prohibition of any controversy which might become a threat to law and order. It was this which led the burgomasters of Amsterdam in 1632 to nominate two commissioners to sit in the consistory, Andries Bicker being one of the first pair.

There was no attempt to impose any doctrine on the church, or to interfere with its discipline over members; but it is recorded that the service in Amsterdam was not to last more than an hour and a half, by order of the burgomasters. It was also action by the city authorities

68, 69 Jan Sweelinck, city organist of Amsterdam, and (right) the organ in the Nieuwe Kerk.

that preserved many of the carillons and organs. The use of organs in church services was anathema to many Calvinists (as it was to some Catholic reformers at the Council of Trent). Not only was their use abandoned, but many wanted them smashed and removed from the churches. But the regents regarded the organs as being the property of the community, and therefore of the magistrates, who continued to pay the organists a salary as city employees. The consistory did not meddle with their appointment, and some were not even Protestants.

At Amsterdam the famous Sweelinck, 'the father of fugue', was organist from 1577 to 1621, with a salary rising eventually to 90 florins a month. He was not required to accompany the psalms, but played voluntaries before and after the service – the 'serious edifying pieces, not motets and thoughtless stuff' that the magistrates of Dordrecht prescribed for their organist – and was responsible also for midweek evening concerts, with singers. These were well attended by Catholics, sectaries and Jews as well as Protestants, and became both a fashion parade and a musical event. Not all approved of this secularization of the organ. A man with the humanistic tastes of Constantijn Huygens could write disapprovingly about what went on between the 'young blood' in the dark corners of the churches during these recitals. Sweelinck had no successors of the same stature, but in this way a tradition was continued until the building of the great baroque organs of the eighteenth century. Long before then the towns had gone over one by one to the use of an organ accompaniment for the psalms, though it was not until 1680 that the burgomasters of Amsterdam prescribed this, and even then it was not enthusiastically received by the consistory.

The Calvinists not unnaturally found this interference by the regents irksome. There were occasions when the regents shared their religious and political sympathies, but there were many others when the regents were much more moderately disposed. The friction caused by differing views about the relationship between church and state was not made less by the fact that the ministers did not come from the same social class as those who filled the city councils; though not drawn from the humblest ranks of society, they were not the younger sons of regent families. In the early seventeenth century the same seems often to have been true of the elders and deacons (and deaconesses, for there were a few women). If Amsterdam is typical, elders and deacons were replaced by co-option, but half of them retired annually and were not eligible for a further year. There were also vergers, sick-visitors, *voorlezers* who read from the Scriptures before the service – and a curious kind of caretaker called a *hondenslager*, or dog-hitter, whose task it was to keep out of church the dogs that were so numerous in Dutch cities; at Amsterdam the first *hondenslager* lost his post for being so drunk that he went to work on children, as well as dogs, with his stick.

All church members were subjected to a close discipline, particularly in relation to the communion service which was held every two months. At each weekly meeting of the consistory the first item on the agenda was always a few cases of discipline. The result was a closely organized community under the leadership of ministers and elders, strongly convinced where its duties lay, hostile to popery and to Spain. In practice this often meant that the princes of Orange had their most faithful followers among the ministers and their congregations, and that these latter did not see eye to eye with the regents of Holland.

Because the regents were more moderate and more tolerant than the stricter Calvinists would have liked, the United Provinces differed considerably from the stereotype of a Calvinist state. English Puritans were sometimes scandalized by the lax observance of the Sabbath that they found in the Dutch cities. Many shops were open, markets held and ships loaded and unloaded. Continued complaints by the church were ignored, nor did the great capitalists pay any attention to the attacks which the synods occasionally made on the taking of usury; under the influence of conservative theologians like Voetius of Utrecht, they might debar even the wife of a money-lender from communion. Calvinism may have contributed to the development of Dutch capitalism by encouraging habits of industry and thrift, but it was only slowly that it modified its conservative social ideas to accommodate the financiers and *rentiers*.

Most important of all, lack of support from the temporal authorities made it impossible for the Calvinists to compel the rest of the Dutch population into conformity with them. In the early days of the Revolt the Sea-Beggars had been guilty of some atrocities, but thereafter there were only vague clamours for action against 'popish abuses'. There were few Catholic martyrs. Only a few brief and local attempts were made to compel attendance at church on pain of a recusancy fine, as in England, and though Catholic worship was officially prohibited, there was no question of penal laws similar to those passed by Elizabethan parliaments against priests celebrating mass. Catholics were supposed not to hold office or serve in the professions, but there were many exceptions to this. Protestantization, if it came at all, would have to come by more peaceful methods.

Protestantization in fact came slowly, and was never complete. In the United Provinces the clergy, at the time of the Revolt, did not conform to Protestantism in the way that many English clergy had done earlier. By the 1580s religious attitudes had become much more clearly defined, and a deliberate change of faith was now necessary. Most of the clergy fled, and a much smaller number of Calvinist ministers had to take their place and preach their doctrines, with the aid of lay sympathizers. It is striking to discover that in Amsterdam there were only two ministers in 1578, six in 1600, and fourteen in 1622. The shortage of trained ministers was only slowly relieved – though it was not to be expected that in a Calvinist system the number of clergy would ever approach its total in pre-Reformation times.

It has sometimes been suggested that the appropriation of charitable endowments by the authorities meant that there was pressure on the poorer classes to conform in order to qualify for relief, but the process of conforming went on so unequally from place to place that it seems dangerous to put too much weight on this. The requirement that schoolmasters should be Protestant, at least nominally, may have been more important in the long run. An increase in the amount of preaching, the habit of conducting worship in the vernacular, the growing identification of Protestantism with the cause of independence, and, with some, the inevitable social advantages of belonging to the established church and worshipping in its buildings, all helped to convert a widespread dissatisfaction with the old faith into a more positive acceptance of the new. The increasing availability of the Scriptures in Dutch also helped, though the pre-Reformation authorities here had never been so fiercely opposed to vernacular Bibles as in England. It was not until 1637 that the States' Bible was published, so called because it was authorized by the States-General, just as the English translation of 1611 had been authorized by James I.

The proportion of Catholics in the seven provinces was gradually reduced; on the other hand, the territories in North Brabant which were conquered by Frederick Henry in and after 1629 were solidly Catholic. They had been exposed to the Counter-Reformation for fifty years, and harsh treatment by their new rulers only served to stiffen their loyalties. Including the minorities which remained in the seven provinces, sustained by missionary priests from outside who were not seriously hindered by the authorities, Catholics still amounted to roughly a third of the total population in the middle of the seventeenth century. In practice Catholic worship was connived at almost everywhere, and not merely in aristocratic households or foreign embassies as in England. *Schuilkerken*, as they were called, were generally known to exist, at first in attics and warehouses, later in houses adapted as chapels. A list of Papist meeting-places presented to the burgomaster of Amsterdam in 1656 contained sixty-two such addresses. There was one in the old Begijnhof, where the nuns had once lived, only a few yards from the entrance to the old church which had been handed over to the English Puritans. Another site still much visited is the 'Ons' Lieve Heer op Solder' church, built for its purpose in 1661 behind an ordinary house façade. (The inside of the church, as it is now seen, dates only from the eighteenth century.)

70 Eighteenth-century interior of the
'Ons' Lieve Heer op Solder' church.

71 Title-page of the first edition
of the States' Bible.

Sometimes the existence of such places was so widely known that
Protestants could direct strangers to them.

Petitions for action against these illegal churches found little
response among the city authorities. What officials did sometimes
expect was a gift of money in return for their connivance. As early as
1594 there were complaints to the States of Holland about this
practice, in Gouda, for instance; and in that same town in 1677 the
burgomasters and Catholics reached a solemn agreement on an
annual payment of 750 guilders. To modern eyes payments of this
kind for the right to worship are abhorrent, but in the Europe of that
age office was everywhere regarded as a legitimate source of profit,
and it was accepted on all sides that exemptions from the operation of
a law should be paid for. It was at least better than the situation in the
Spanish Netherlands, where no Protestantism was allowed at all.

This practical indulgence towards Catholics is the more remarkable
when it is considered that the Republic was engaged in a life-and-death

struggle with the leading Catholic power. Catholics were not a dangerous fifth column. Later, in 1672–73, Louis XIV's armies occupied Utrecht, and under his protection Catholic services were once more held in the Dom for nearly eighteen months, but this led neither to a sympathetic response to the invaders from Dutch Catholics, nor to savage anti-Papist reprisals when the French had departed. Only in 1747 did another French invasion lead to anti-Papist riots in the border town of Bergen-op-Zoom. This is one sign that, whatever indulgence there might be, the two faiths did not grow together as time passed. Local Protestant and Catholic communities tended to grow more stubborn and more exclusive. The Catholics of Vollendam and the Protestants of Marken might live peacefully near to one another, but they 'kept themselves to themselves'. And in time the Catholics were bound to resent their inferior legal position and their exclusion from power.

More startling still to contemporaries was the toleration granted to a variety of sectaries. 'I believe in this street where I lodge,' wrote James Howell, 'there be well near as many religions as there be houses; for one neighbour knows not, nor cares not much what religion the other is of, so that the number of conventicles exceed the number of churches here. And let this country call itself as long as it will, the United Provinces one way, I am persuaded in this point,

72 Cornelis Anslo, Mennonite preacher: drawing by Rembrandt.

there's no place so disunited.' Some observers, like Marvell, and later many Tories, derided this toleration; others admired it and linked it with Dutch success in trade. Merchants who sought profit in any land where it was to be found irrespective of its religion, and those who wanted to attract strangers to the markets of Amsterdam, were unlikely to risk any religious bars to commerce. Yet it would not be fair to put down the policy of the regents simply to a calculation of profit and loss; it represented a genuine attitude of mind which hated persecution and found it unreasonable.

The Remonstrants, as a group originally within the official Calvinist church, presented special problems, political as well as religious, and will be treated separately. The most numerous of the sects, the Mennonites, those Anabaptists who followed the peaceful teaching of Menno Simons (1492–1559), were permitted to organize themselves in congregations, and even their difficulties about bearing arms and swearing oaths were taken into account. Rembrandt painted one of their best-known preachers, Cornelis Anslo, and since he had plenty of opportunity for contact with them through Saskia's uncle, Hendrick Uylenburgh, it has been suggested that they may have influenced his Biblical paintings. Lutherans were easily accepted and in 1630 were permitted to build a church, of distinctive design, on the Singel in Amsterdam. It would be tedious to list all the minor sects, but it is necessary to stress that, whereas in England in the 1640s the sectaries reacted against an oppressive Establishment by developing

73 The Lutheran church, Amsterdam.

radical political ideas, in the Dutch Republic they looked to the regents for indulgence and protection from the orthodox Calvinists who sometimes petitioned against them. They were a peaceful, not a revolutionary element in society.

Most remarkable was the existence of a large Jewish community in Amsterdam, living in a Jewish quarter, not a ghetto, and permitted to worship in public synagogues from 1597. They included both Sephardim from Portugal and Spain, and Ashkenazim from Germany and Poland. Their importance in the development of Amsterdam capitalism has sometimes been exaggerated, and there were many poor among them as well as some moderately well-to-do. Rabbi Manasseh ben Israel was well known and was consulted by Calvinist Old Testament scholars; Rembrandt, who lived opposite his house in Jodenbreestraat, had many opportunities to observe Jews and use them as models, and was probably the first artist to derive his idea of Christ from a personal study of them. By 1675 the Portuguese Jews were wealthy enough to build a splendid new synagogue, though it was not until 1796 that they were given full citizenship.

Toleration, which we all nowadays accept as an ideal, carries several different meanings. In the sense of freedom of private cons-

74 Samuel Manasseh ben Israel: portrait by Govaert Flinck, 1637.

75 Emanuel de Witte's view of the Portuguese synagogue, its style fully in keeping with
contemporary Dutch classicism.

cience it was a founding principle of the Union and was virtually *Toleration*
complete in the seventeenth-century Dutch Republic. A long intellectual tradition from Erasmus onwards opposed persecution merely
for holding heretical beliefs. When Dirk Coornhert declared in 1578,

'I hold for brethren all those godly men who hold Christ for their corner-stone, whether they be priests, monks, Baptists, Reformed or Lutherans', he was putting this belief much more positively than many Calvinists liked, and was regarded by them as a dangerous free-thinker. Nonetheless, the five syndics who look out at us from Rembrandt's masterpiece are a perpetual reminder that diversity of belief did exist among colleagues, for two were Calvinist, two Catholic and one a Mennonite.

In its second sense, toleration can mean freedom of worship. The Republic did not adopt this as a theoretical principle, and Calvinist preachers frequently called for action against Papist and sectarian congregations, but in practice they were very rarely interfered with by the authorities after the first years of the Revolt. In the third sense, implying equality of legal status for men of all persuasions, toleration certainly did not exist, though there were no tithes or church rates for non-members of the official church, and civil marriage at the town hall was valid for all. The exclusion of non-Calvinists from office was not invariably maintained, but this and other restrictions, particularly on Catholics, weighed more heavily as time went on.

In comparison with other states there was a remarkable variety of religious belief, and along with it a remarkable degree of intellectual freedom. Foreign observers sometimes thought that the Dutch were one-third adherents of the Reformed church, one-third Catholic and one-third dissenters or free-thinkers. This division may be too convenient to be absolutely accurate, and it may do less than justice to the influence which Calvinism came to wield even over non-members.

76 View of the pulpit in the Portuguese synagogue, 1675.

77 Rembrandt's *The Syndics of the Cloth Hall.*

In the process of time it stiffened habits of sobriety, hard work and toughness in the face of danger in a way which cannot, in the nature of things, be measured; and the combination of Calvinist orthodoxy and practical indulgence had its effect even upon Catholics, so that Dutch Catholicism is now unlike that of any other part of Europe.

Even witches benefited from the enlightened outlook of the political authorities. Persecution ceased here earlier than in other European countries. No witches were judicially executed after 1595, and the last trial in Holland, ending in acquittal, took place in 1610. Of course Calvinists believed generally in the existence of witchcraft – was it not to be found in the Scriptures? – but there was no encouragement to put individual old women on trial. In 1691 Baltasar Bekker created a sensation by publishing a book, *De Betoverde Wereld* ('The World Bewitched'), directed against belief in the activity of supernatural forces in the world. He was removed from his ministry in the church – but the civic authorities went on paying his salary.

II DUTCH CIVILIZATION

The preceding pages will have given some idea of the human, material and spiritual resources of the Dutch, if they were given time to exploit them. But in the first instance everything depended upon their ability to beat back the military forces of the Spaniards. In retrospect their success may seem easier than was the case – perhaps even 'inevitable'. In reality the margin was small in the first decade after the Union of Utrecht. The political, economic and intellectual development of Europe might well have been altered by a Spanish victory.

In the early 1580s, a new Spanish Governor-General in Brussels, the Duke of Parma, had, through a combination of political and military skill, enjoyed a remarkable success in winning back large areas of the South for Philip II. This culminated in the capture of Antwerp in 1585 after a siege lasting over a year. The Dutch, on the other hand, suffered in the assassination of William the Silent the loss of the man whose qualities as a political leader had been recognized by Philip's action in putting a price upon his head. It seemed unlikely that anyone else could perform so well the task of persuading the different local bodies to work together in the general interest.

The Dutch were saved partly through their own efforts – through the naval and financial strength already described – and partly by a combination of favourable circumstances. The number of walled cities and the waterways which intersected the North meant that Parma's formidable armies could not sweep through the opposition in one or two campaigns with battles in open country; the process would take time, and concentration by Philip II on this one objective to the exclusion of others. But this he did not give. He allowed himself to be diverted, first to the conflict with England and the Armada and then in 1590 and 1592 to campaigning in France to help the Catholic League. The result was that by 1596 Philip was bankrupt, while the States-General, acting as an independent power, were in alliance with Henry of Navarre, as well as Elizabeth of England: a remarkable reversal of fortune in a few years.

In the meantime the Dutch had made good use of their respite. Determination to survive had got the better of their internal jealousies. At times the stresses had been severe, notably when Leicester (at the head of some English forces) had become exasperated by what he thought of as the dilatoriness and half-heartedness of the regents. He had appealed to the Calvinists and lower classes in Utrecht and elsewhere, in order to bring about a more unitary form of government based on popular sovereignty and religious orthodoxy. By the middle of the 1590s this danger had faded. Decentralization and oligarchy had triumphed. The regents had proved able to hold their own against Spain, and were in firm control of the towns, the States of Holland and the States-General, and the great economic leap forward had begun.

The person most responsible for this was the Advocate, Jan van Oldenbarnevelt, a statesman of European stature, able to reconcile the demands of central authority and provincial autonomy, and possessing great intelligence, and powers of hard work, persuasiveness and

78 Jan van Oldenbarnevelt:
Advocate of Holland and
Remonstrant sympathizer,
he was judicially murdered
by Prince Maurice in 1619.

diplomatic skill. At the same time William the Silent's second son, Maurice of Nassau, had become stadholder of five of the seven provinces of the Union and a soldier of note. He and his cousin, William Louis, the stadholder of Friesland and Groningen, were both interested in new and more scientific methods of warfare, in engineering and fortification. Conditions in the Low Countries were such that progress had to be made by sieges rather than battles, and an expertise was now developed which lasted to the time of Coehoorn, the military engineer who was Vauban's great rival at the end of the seventeenth century. Soldiers from other Protestant countries came to learn their trade in Maurice's armies. The battle of Nieuwpoort (1600) showed that they were a match for the foremost army in Europe.

By 1609 the Spaniards were ready, not to admit defeat, cut their losses and recognize the independence of the northern provinces, but at least to sign a Twelve Years' Truce with them. This success was not gained without controversies much more serious than the previous inter-provincial disputes about contributions to the common effort. Oldenbarnevelt himself went over late to the peace party, believing that war was still almost the only bond between the provinces. Others opposed the truce, from a mixture of Calvinist zeal against Popery and desire for gain. Zeeland fitted out many privateers to prey on enemy shipping. The East India Company wished to continue to break open the Portuguese grip on the Spice Islands. The promoters of a new West India Company were the most bellicose of all; its propagandists, many of them refugees from the South, wanted not a peaceful trading company, but one which would attack the Spanish position in the New World, and seize its gold and silver as well as its trade. They were particularly strong in Amsterdam. Maurice too, a soldier and personally ambitious, was reluctant; but in the end he allowed himself to be persuaded, and used his own influence to persuade Zeeland to accept the truce. But, since it was only a truce and not a peace, the central questions of policy were not resolved, and at the same time religious problems were appearing which would aggravate the constitutional and foreign policy difficulties.

At the centre of Calvinist belief was a conviction of the utter depravity of human nature and of man's complete inability to contribute in any way, whether by good works, religious observance or personal faith, to his own salvation. Salvation was the result solely of the operation of divine grace, and each soul was predestined to eternal

79, 80 Remonstrant and Counter-Remonstrant opponents: Jacobus Arminius and (right) Franciscus Gomarus.

bliss or damnation. Once a breathing-space had been won from the threat of Popery, against which these doctrines represented a reaction, their rigidity was almost bound to be called in question. By its very nature divine grace was a mystery on which theologians were likely to disagree. Did the divine decree date from before the Fall, in which case it could be argued that God was responsible for the creation of sin, or from after the Fall, in which case it could be argued that this was a breach of His omnipotence? Arminius, who became a professor at Leiden in 1603, tended to give rather more scope to the human will though he maintained that his doctrines did not differ fundamentally from the orthodox ones; his followers went further. Gomarus, also a professor at Leiden, was unbending in his defence of orthodoxy, and in his view that no breach in the unity of the church's doctrine could be permitted, lest it open the way for Popery. Since the students of the two men were seeking calls to ministries, and since Arminius was a popular teacher, this could not remain simply an academic dispute. It became a controversy to be thrashed out from every pulpit; and though political considerations came to be mixed up in it, the volume of pamphlet literature which was produced shows clearly that men were passionately concerned with the doctrinal problems. Only recently the Calvinist cause had been fighting for its very life, and this no doubt made the defenders of orthodoxy more vehement than they might otherwise have been.

The Arminians were never more than a minority group, but they sought to counterbalance this by appealing to the political authorities for protection. A Remonstrance to the States of Holland in 1610 set out their views on predestination, pleaded for freedom to argue for the revision of points in the Heidelberg Catechism, the standard formulary of Calvinist beliefs, and maintained that the States had authority in spiritual as well as temporal matters. As a result they became known as Remonstrants, and their opponents as Counter-Remonstrants.

A majority of the States of Holland and its constituent towns was composed of regents who, if they did not actively sympathize with Remonstrant ideas, were inclined towards tolerant views and strongly disinclined to become simply the secular arm of an intolerant church. But their main concern was to damp down controversy in the interests of peace and harmony. The question was, how was this to be done? Since the church in each town was organized as one congregation with one consistory, the matter could not be dealt with by separation of the two parties into different buildings. The States therefore tried to order preachers to refrain from discussing the points at issue, and punished clergy who disregarded this ban. This led the orthodox clergy, not unnaturally, to protest against interference by political authorities in the affairs of the church, and to demand a different kind of freedom from that desired by the Remonstrants (though eventually they were not averse from using the temporal power to crush their opponents). Some, banned from preaching in the towns, led crowds of sympathizers to the churches in the suburbs, and disorders grew.

The struggle of a minority in the church to maintain itself, and of the majority to crush it, had thus raised the wider issue of the relations between church and state. Soon there arose the additional problem of the relations between the States-General and the provincial States, for a majority of the seven provinces in the States-General was prepared to call a national synod to consider the doctrinal issue, while a majority of the States of Holland and Utrecht, knowing that the

81 Construction of the Remonstrant Church in Amsterdam in 1640: despite official Counter-Remonstrant dominance, Remonstrant ideals retained considerable influence.

Remonstrants would be in a minority at such a synod, argued that the consent of all seven provinces was necessary for this. Finally, in 1617, the States of Holland, led by Oldenbarnevelt, passed the 'Sharp Resolution'. This was in effect a declaration of provincial sovereignty in religion, and it included a decision to empower the cities to raise a special force of *waardgelders*, taking an oath of allegiance only to the States of Holland, with no mention of the Captain-General.

By this time, however, Maurice had decided to take a hand. His personal life was far from being a model of Calvinistic godliness, and his interest in the doctrinal issue was small. He is said to have remarked that he did not know whether predestination was blue or green, but he now proceeded, as it were, to make it Orange. He had grown

off van syn Pr. Excell. Mauritius.
assau Prince van Orangen.

T'HOF VAN HOLLANDT

de Hof Kerck

de graote Saelle

82 The execution of Jan van Oldenbarnevelt, from an anonymous contemporary engraving.

hostile to the tutelage of Oldenbarnevelt, and disliked both the Truce of 1609 and the smaller scope which was his in peacetime. He may also have been conscious of the approach of the year 1621, when the Truce would expire; unless some kind of unity could be restored to the United Provinces, they would be helpless to resist Spain. Spurred on by his cousin William Louis, he intervened with decisive effect, claiming to act in support of the authority of the States-General. Oldenbarnevelt's sense of political realism had deserted him. His position was fatally weakened by the fact that the States of Holland were not themselves united; among other towns, Amsterdam had a Counter-Remonstrant majority on its council, pressing for a strong Calvinist policy at home and abroad (where the promoters of an anti-Spanish West India Company were still active). Maurice was able to pick off the opposing towns one by one.

Oldenbarnevelt was tried by a special tribunal consisting of his personal enemies, and found guilty of treason. Perhaps as the outcome of years of frustration, perhaps because he could not believe that after more than thirty years of service the old man's influence was really at an end, perhaps because he felt that an act of power was needed to crush his opponents, Maurice refused to pardon his former ally, and Oldenbarnevelt went to the scaffold. It is a blot on the usually peaceful record of Dutch politics; yet this was the only bloodshed. One of Oldenbarnevelt's lieutenants, the great Grotius, was imprisoned for two years until he escaped from the castle of Loevestein in a chest supposed to contain books, to spend most of the rest of his life in Paris. Religious orthodoxy was affirmed at the famous Synod of Dort.

In the hour of Calvinist triumph, however, there was no thought of the church becoming more independent than before. The synod itself was held 'under the authority of their High Mightinesses the States-General'; it was attended by eighteen lay representatives of the States-General to see that the interests of the secular power were not overlooked; and there was no provision made for regular meetings in the future. The Calvinists were content to enjoy the support of the state in eliminating their opponents. The Remonstrants appeared as defendants, rather than fellow-members of the synod; the result of the theological deliberations was a foregone conclusion, and some 200 of them were deprived of their ministries. The States-

83 The castle of Loevestein, where Grotius was imprisoned.

t'Huys te
LOVENSTEYN

General resolved that they should be allowed a choice between keeping silence with half a year's salary and banishment, and about eighty of them, led by Uytenbogaert and Episcopius, chose the latter. Remonstrant conventicles were officially prohibited.

This departure from the normal Dutch tolerance did not last long once it became clear that the only ambition of the Remonstrants was to remain a sect, and not to reverse the decision of Dort. Frederick Henry, who succeeded as stadholder in 1625, had known and respected Uytenbogaert, and was not by nature a persecutor; and after the resumption of a successful war with Spain (and the foundation at last of a West India Company), national unity was restored and the political need for orthodoxy at all costs no longer existed. By 1630 there were Remonstrant churches in Amsterdam and Rotterdam, and by 1632 there was even an academy in Amsterdam which was to develop into a university. Petitions for action against them were evaded by the magistrates, who came to sympathize more with the flexible and tolerant ideals of the Remonstrants – and their respect for political authority – than with the extremist zeal of the orthodox Calvinists. A generation earlier the Counter-Remonstrants had ruled Amsterdam, but from about 1627 Nicolaes Tulp was definitely one of a minority among the regents.

For the rest of the seventeenth century the Remonstrants were only a small group, but they played a far more important part in Dutch intellectual life than mere numbers would suggest, and their influence, in accordance with the needs of their position, was always liberal,

84, 85 Opposite: Hugo Grotius
and Simon Episcopius,
Remonstrant refugees from Holland.

86 John Locke, who found
political refuge in
the Netherlands
between 1683 and 1689.

tolerant and opposed to credal rigidities – *in necessariis unitas, in non necessariis libertas, in utrisque caritas* ('In essentials unity, in doubtful matters liberty, in all things charity'). Episcopius defended toleration except for blasphemy. Truth, which was the strongest support of the church, would not suffer from toleration, whereas intolerance would stifle liberty of conscience, hinder reform and stimulate hypocrisy. It was not, he argued, the magistrates' duty to impose a particular view: 'Religion must be defended not by slaying but by admonishing, not by ferocity but by patience, not by crime but by faith.'

It has been suggested that some of the English Independents were directly inspired by Remonstrant principles, and that Philip Nye, who had experience of religious conditions in the Netherlands before he opposed the Presbyterians in the Westminster Assembly, developed theories closely related to Episcopius's arguments. A complete edition of Episcopius was published in England in 1678; and when John Locke took refuge in the Netherlands in the 1680s, one of his several Remonstrant friends was van Limborch, Professor of Theology at the Academy in Amsterdam, whose wife was Episcopius's niece. It is also noteworthy that the same Academy, in the middle of the seventeenth century, contained some of the strongest supporters of Cartesian ideas (which led to unusually bitter disputes in the Republic, precisely because the freedom of the press permitted greater controversy).

If the Remonstrants won a measure of acceptance (though many Calvinists grudged it) and contributed to the intellectual life of the

87 Velazquez's *The Surrender of Breda*.

Republic in this way, the crisis of 1618 nevertheless left its mark on Dutch life. The tensions between the 'libertine' magistrates of the cities and the Calvinism of much of the populace, between the States of Holland and the States-General, and between the regents and the House of Orange, were not finally resolved; and in the long run the judicial murder of Oldenbarnevelt did not help to resolve them. For some time, indeed, the successes of Frederick Henry hid these problems. Taking over from Maurice in 1625, the year in which Spain won one of its few victories – celebrated by Velazquez in his *Surrender of Breda* – Frederick Henry took 's Hertogenbosch, Tilburg and Maastricht and eventually recaptured Breda. The Catholic provinces of

88, 89, 90 War against Spain: (above) silver salt-cellar commemorating the successful siege of 's Hertogen-bosch, 1629; (right) silver beaker showing the recapture of Breda, 1637; (below) the surrender of Hulst to Frederick Henry, 1645.

the South failed to rise in rebellion against Spain, but the North was safe. By this time a separate Dutch nationality clearly existed, and at Münster in 1648 Spain at last recognized its independence.

But the very coming-of-age of the Dutch state was accompanied by the revival of dissensions. Each of the seven provinces had sent its own delegation to Münster, accompanied by ladies who had to be fêted and given suitable gifts by Spain to make the course of diplomacy proceed more smoothly. Back in the Netherlands there were reams of propaganda for and against reaching terms with the old enemy. When the time came for the treaty on 30 January 1648, the Utrecht ambassador refused to sign, and the treaty was therefore strictly contrary to the terms of the Union. The Zeeland representative was also ordered to stay away from the ceremony of ratification, which was not quite the great national occasion which might appear from the famous painting by ter Borch.

91 *The Swearing of the Oath of Ratification of the Treaty of Münster*, by Gerard ter Borch. The Netherlands delegates stand, hands raised, round the centre table: the Spanish delegates are on their left.

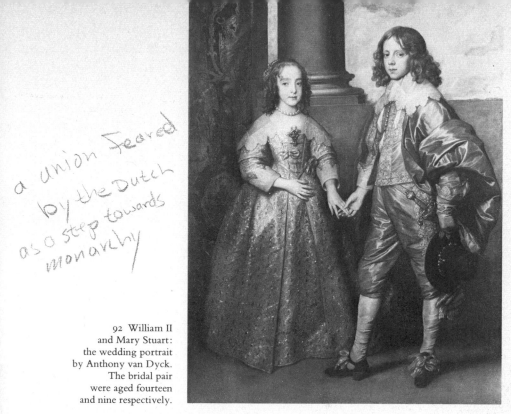

a union feared by the Dutch as a step towards monarchy

92 William II
and Mary Stuart:
the wedding portrait
by Anthony van Dyck.
The bridal pair
were aged fourteen
and nine respectively.

Amsterdam, however, which had been fiercely bellicose at the beginning of the century, was now firmly in the peace party. In the view of the majority of the regents the war with Spain no longer served any political purpose; peace would suit their trading interests and therefore the prosperity of the whole of the Union. In addition, there was widespread suspicion of the aims of the princes of Orange. Under Frederick Henry monarchical tendencies had increased, though all the constitutional forms were preserved, and in 1641 he was successful in marrying his son William into the royal House of Stuart. To some, all this was a natural step on a road taken by other states, and to be welcomed as a way of strengthening national unity. To others it was unwelcome, because it was feared, with much justification, that the princes would try to use Dutch resources to further their own dynastic interests, and entangle the Republic in the collapsing fortunes of their Stuart relatives.

There were also disputes about the degree of disarmament after peace had been signed, with Amsterdam ever more prominent in

93 William II advances to attack the rebellious city of Amsterdam on 1 August 1650: from the painting by Johannes Lingelbach.

opposing William II (who succeeded his father in 1647). Eventually, in 1650, William planned an armed *coup* against the city, together with the imprisonment of some of his leading opponents in the castle of Loevestein. His troops went astray in the darkness, but the trade of Amsterdam could not stand the possibility of a blockade, and the brothers Bicker found it wiser to step down from the City Council than to hold out. William might have triumphed, but the crisis was resolved by his sudden death from smallpox. Since his son, William III, was a posthumous child, there followed a stadholderless period, dominated by Johan de Witt, who became Grand Pensionary in 1653. Unfortunately the sequence could not be broken here. With the memory of 1650 in his mind, de Witt was bound to make every effort to prevent young William from ever being in a position to repeat the *coup*, perhaps with the aid of his English relatives; William, on the other hand, was bound to resent his exclusion from the offices which his father and grandfather had held. The result was the tragedy of 1672.

It was against this background of political events that the writers, artists and scientists did their creative work.

LECTURES AND BOOKS

Before the Revolt, the Florentine Guicciardini had declared that nearly all Netherlands peasants could read and write. It would be dangerous to take this statement too literally, but there can be no doubt that the level of education was relatively high. The Revolt itself did little harm to it in the northern provinces. Except in the early years, the provinces of Holland and Zeeland saw little fighting, and while England, France, Germany and Italy all had to live through periods of civil war and invasion, the towns of Holland were free from disturbance apart from the years 1672–73. Internal peace, growing prosperity and leisure, the expanding urban communities, humanistic traditions and the encouragement always given to education by Calvinism: here were suitable conditions for development, and they were fostered by enlightened regents, and the absence of a political authority capable of controlling the flow of ideas.

In 1575 the University of Leiden was founded and endowed from the lands of the dissolved Abbey of Egmond. Eventually, of course, other provinces had to have their own (notably Utrecht, in 1636); but Leiden rapidly acquired a unique position among the Protestant

94 View of the University in 1625.

universities of Europe, and attracted students from many other
countries. It had pastors among its professors and would-be pastors
among its students, but no tests of religious orthodoxy were required –
simply a declaration of willingness to obey the university statutes.
It was not closely governed by the church, but in effect by two
curators, chosen by the States of Holland, and the four burgomasters
of the city, who appointed and dismissed professors, while internally
the Rector Magnificus held sway.

From the beginning the choice of professors was enterprising;
foreigners as well as Dutchmen were invited, with comparatively
high salaries and generous conditions as inducements. Galileo was
invited at one time, but did not accept. The envoys who went to
invite Joseph Scaliger, the French classical scholar, were offered a
bonus if they were successful, and Scaliger, whom Mark Pattison
once described as 'the greatest scholar of modern times' and 'the most
richly stored intellect which ever spent itself in acquiring knowledge',
did come, though when he arrived he thought Leiden 'a swamp within
a swamp'. Of the native Dutchmen who were appointed to chairs,

95 Willibrord Snellius,
mathematician
and astronomer.

97 The Botanical Garden at
the University.

96 A student in his room.

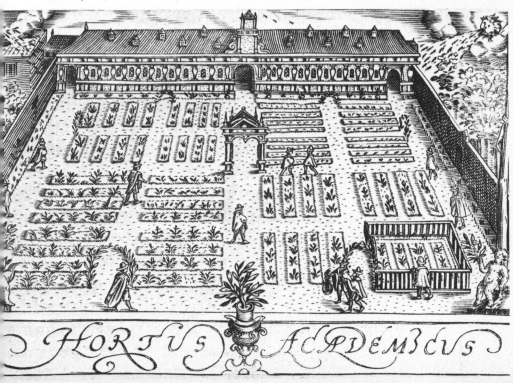

HORTVS ACADEMICVS

some, like the classicist, philologist, literary critic and poet, Daniel Heinsius, were keen Calvinists; but the curators were quite capable of selecting Arminius (with an official salary of 1,200 florins, plus 150 for the rent of a house) to balance Gomarus, and, in spite of the harassment of Arminius, the spirit of relatively free inquiry which existed attracted both teachers and students. Only in the year of the Synod of Dort was this marred, when two curators and two professors were dismissed. Converted Jews were admitted as *docent* – in Hebrew and Arabic.

The university was also enlightened in its encouragement of new fields of study. Scaliger's interest in examining Chaldean and Arabic sources for dates and other materials for ecclesiastical history helped to found Leiden's reputation for the study of oriental languages; Golius too, originally a mathematician and astronomer who sought information from Arabic literature, became an orientalist of European reputation. The study of Islam fitted in well with the growth of Dutch trading interests in the Levant. Equally, sea-captains from far across the world could bring specimens for the Botanical Garden, which was one of the first in northern Europe (1587), and had value both for botanists and in medicine – pure and applied science were never very far apart. An observatory was built in 1632 for the mathematician and astronomer Willibrord Snellius, 'the father of triangulation'; under the statutes it was to be open to the public.

Other more material inducements were offered. Professors and students were allowed 40 gallons of wine a year each, and half a barrel of beer per month, free of excise duty. But students were expected to be able to hold this alarming quantity of drink: a French traveller reported in 1662 that they were forbidden to duel or 'faire la nuit des insolences, et de casser les vitres des bourgeois', and he thought them very orderly.

As a result, students came to Leiden from all over Europe – mainly from Protestant countries, though Catholics also could matriculate and take degrees. In the second quarter of the seventeenth century, when numbers were greatest, there was an average annual enrolment of 443 new students, of whom 52 per cent came from outside the United Provinces. The number of English-speaking students was at its height in the decade 1640–49, when it totalled exactly 300. Some of them, like John Evelyn, did not stay very long; others no doubt enrolled for the sake of the beer. Some English visitors thought the university compared poorly with their own Oxford. In the words of James Howell, 'To compare their university to yours, were to cast New Inn in counterscale with Christ Church College, or the alms-houses on Tower Hill to Sutton's Hospital. Here are no colleges at all, God wot (but one for the Dutch) nor scarce the face of an University . . . all the students are Oppidans. A small time and less learning will suffice to make one a graduate; nor are those formalities of habits, and other decencies here, as with you. . . .' But some who did not conform to the Church of England thought otherwise; and also there was a steady flow of medical students, from Sir Thomas Browne to Oliver Goldsmith – including Lemuel Gulliver.

The period in the 1720s when Swift wrote *Gulliver's Travels* was the time when the reputation of the Leiden medical school was at its height. Its fame dated back to the early seventeenth century, when, apart from Padua, the university's Anatomical Theatre had been the only place where the human body was publicly dissected for the sake of teaching. But there was no one at that time of the repute later gained by Herman Boerhaave (1666–1738). For many years he held three chairs, those of botany, chemistry and medicine. He lectured to his medical students on all three subjects with great assiduity, and enjoyed remarkable popularity as a teacher, his students going half an hour early to be sure of a place at his lectures. Since some were at 7 a.m. and all were in Latin, this was no small tribute. His *Institutiones Medicae*, published in 1707, was essentially a text-book for his courses, but it was soon in use throughout western Europe, with pirated editions and translations into English, French and German. His greatest claim to fame was his skill in clinical teaching, which had not previously received much attention in medical education; he taught twice a week in the St Cecilia Hospital, and his pupils must have killed fewer patients as a result. When Peter the Great visited Leiden in 1715, he moored his yacht in the Rapenburg canal in front of the University, and sent a messenger to ask the famous professor when it would be convenient to receive him. Boerhaave tactfully left the time to the Tsar, who fixed 5 a.m. The two men talked together for two hours and visited the Botanical Garden (of which Boerhaave was curator), before the Tsar went in search of the other professors, waiting in their lecture-rooms, and the Anatomical Theatre.

Between 1701 and Boerhaave's death in 1738, 1,919 students matriculated in medicine, including 659 from English-speaking

98 Herman Boerhaave,
world-famous professor
and teacher of medicine.

countries. A group of nine, including Alexander Monro, who matriculated between 1718 and 1721, was largely responsible for the development of the Edinburgh medical school; van Swieten founded an equally famous school at Vienna, and others went to Göttingen and Berlin.

Leiden University possessed one other great asset in its printing-press. From soon after its foundation this was in the hands of the Elseviers. Lodewijk Elsevier was yet another *émigré* from the South who, having worked for Plantin, came to Leiden in 1580, and after some years established himself there as bookseller and then printer. He was by no means the only one in Leiden (no less than sixty-one are recorded there between 1600 and 1624), but he rapidly won a unique reputation for the production of books for the scholar, and some of his children and grandchildren set up branches in The Hague, Utrecht and especially Amsterdam. Some of his books were editions of the classics – duodecimo size, the cheap pocket editions of their day, and notable for their clarity of type. They included some to suit Leiden's special interest in Oriental languages, until the special type was bought by the Oxford university press in the eighteenth century. But there were books on every field of scholarship,

A contemporary print shows a class in the Anatomical Theatre at Leiden.

'unique to Europe

GULIELMI PISONIS
MEDICI AMSTELAEDAMENSIS
DE
INDIAE UTRIUSQUE
RE NATURALI ET MEDICA
LIBRI QUATUORDECIM,
Quorum contenta pagina sequens
exhibet.

AMSTELAEDAMI,
Apud Ludovicum et Danielem
ELZEVIRIOS.
A°. cIɔ Iɔ c LVIII.

theological, philological, historical and scientific, medical and literary. The early Elseviers in Leiden were strong Calvinists, like many first-generation *émigrés*, and did not publish Grotius or Descartes; but in the second half of the seventeenth century the Amsterdam branch had much more catholic tastes, printing alike Descartes and his opponents, Grotius and Selden, Milton and Salmasius, Hobbes and Pascal. As the century proceeded, the proportion of books in Dutch and French increased at the expense of those in Latin.

The Elseviers, however, were only the most distinguished among a host of printers and publishers. In Amsterdam alone, in the last quarter of the seventeenth century, 273 are recorded; and it has even been suggested that over the whole century more books were printed in the Netherlands than in all the rest of Europe put together. This is the kind of guess which is scarcely capable of statistical proof, but when the vast output, ranging from the thickest of folios to the most ephemeral pamphlet and news-sheet, is taken into consideration, it is not so wild as it seems. Foreigners brought their writings to be printed in the Dutch Republic to avoid the attention of their own censorship – notably in the reign of Charles I. Laud complained in 1632 that the Dutch, printing more accurate texts on better paper and in clearer type, were able to sell Geneva Bibles in England eighteenpence cheaper than their English competitors.

Success of this sort was the result of a good eye for economic opportunity, in both the export and the home market, and of an efficient paper industry; but it also depended on the wide freedom of publication. It would be wrong to claim that this freedom was absolute, for there were printing regulations which varied, characteristically, from city to city, and extraordinary prosecutions like that of the Koerbaghs, for publishing the view that Christ was not God, but merely a great preacher. The States-General, however, had no censors whose official approval had to be obtained. Occasionally a foreign power might complain about something offensive – as when James I complained about Brewster's press at Leiden – or synods might protest against a treatise which smacked of Socinianism; then the city might respond with an official ban on the publication (if the pressure could not be evaded by delay). But the writer never had much to fear personally, unlike the English Puritans Prynne, Bastwick and Burton, who in 1637 were punished by mutilation for their opposition to the religious policy of the Crown. On the rare occasions when a ban was imposed, there was no authority with the zeal or the efficiency of the Inquisition to search for forbidden books; on the contrary, when one city could connive at their sale no longer, author and books could go to the next. Usually the regents were inclined to indulgence, both from their general attitude of mind and because they realized the economic advantage to be derived from the sale of books and pamphlets.

The most important works to be honoured with a ban were those of Spinoza. It may fairly be argued that it is not easy to tell where else they would have been published at all in the 1670s, and that the very fact that they appeared reflects credit on the Dutch; and if they passed rapidly into oblivion for a century, this can hardly be put down to the effectiveness of the ban. Still, this important exception is a reminder that the freedom was not complete. What is true is that the norm prevailing was different from that in other parts of Europe, and that this was due to a combination of enlightenment and the absence of strong central political institutions, which might have developed ambitions to control thought.

Amsterdam was the greatest international book-market in Europe; but, besides their foreign sales, the publishers obviously catered for a large reading public in the Dutch cities themselves, and they did this by supplying a vastly increased number of books in the Dutch language. Some authors, like the versatile Constantijn Huygens, wrote in both Latin and Dutch, but the first half of the seventeenth century is notable for the development of a vernacular literature. It produced prose writers like Hooft, the historian; playwrights – for there was a theatre, in spite of Calvinist complaints – like Bredero, whose comedies are still performed; and others who are notable in Dutch literary history, but who have never made their mark in Europe as a whole.

How far this has been due to the fact that they wrote in a little-known language it is not easy to say: the ease with which Dutch men of letters adopted French in the eighteenth century suggests awareness of this problem of language, and not merely subservience to French models. But these writers have been little translated. It is difficult to imagine anyone wishing to translate long stretches of the work of Jacob Cats (1577–1660), whose didactic, homely verse – 'typically Dutch', we are told – was so popular with Dutch readers from the seventeenth century to the twentieth. If it is true that an illustrated edition of Cats had sold 50,000 copies by 1655, this is less

101, 102 Contemporary authors: Joost van den Vondel and Constantijn Huygens.

an indication of the quality of his poetry than of the extent of the Dutch reading public. It is rather more surprising that Vondel (1587–1679) has received little attention in other countries, other than the suggestion by Edmund Gosse and George Edmundson that Milton was acquainted with his *Lucifer* before writing *Paradise Lost*. (*Lucifer* was banned after its first performance on the stage because, like Milton's epic, it was said to show Satan in a too favourable light.) Only in this connection has it been – rather woodenly – translated. It is true that Vondel's poetic dramas are more remarkable for richness of language than for strength of plot or subtlety of characterization. His qualities are not those which would be most likely to survive translation. At all events, whereas Vondel would have been widely recognized as one of the great classical poets if he had written in French, the fact that he wrote in Dutch meant that he was less well known in European literary circles than he deserved.

The two greatest writers even of the Dutch 'Golden Age', Grotius and Spinoza, still wrote in Latin to appeal to the world of international scholarship, though Grotius – even the name is commonly

Latinized – also wrote many lines of verse in Dutch. During his imprisonment in the castle of Loevestein after the suppression of the Remonstrants in 1619, he set out to defend *The Truth of the Christian Religion* in Dutch rhyme for Dutch sailors to carry God's message through the world. But the fact that he wrote in Dutch excited some surprise, and it was only the Latin edition of 1627 and later translations into many languages that gave the work wide currency as a gentle, uncontroversial, mildly rational defence of an undogmatic Christianity which would refuse toleration only to those who denied the existence of God and the immortality of the soul – Grotius's Remonstrant antecedents are easy to discern. His two great works on international law, the *Mare Liberum* and the *De Jure Belli ac Pacis*, reflect the practical concern of one who took an active part in politics himself, as Pensionary of Rotterdam and ambassador – Grotius was anything but an 'ivory tower' thinker – but their very subject and purpose meant it was inconceivable that they should first appear in any language but Latin. So far as Spinoza was concerned, the Dutch vocabulary was far less suited to the needs of his philosophical thought than Latin.

Grotius and Spinoza, therefore, became great international figures in a way that others, using Dutch, could not hope to do, and they passed into the general current of European thought on international law and philosophy. Yet their writings bear unmistakable signs of the Dutch background against which they wrote. Grotius's argument that the seas should be free for the navigation and trade of all nations sprang from a denial of Portuguese claims in the East Indies, and his assertion that fishing ought to be free from tolls from the Dutch case in current disputes with James I. To deny that any country could arrogate to itself sovereignty over the sea suited the needs of Dutch trade – at least in European waters: for a time came when the Dutch themselves tried to exclude others from the East Indies, and the English argued the freedom of the seas in that area against the author of *Mare Liberum*, on embassy in London! *De Jure Belli* reflected the interests of a society of traders who were not pacifists, but who desired to restrain an international lawlessness which could only dislocate their commerce. A just war could be fought for purposes of defence, recovery of property, or for the punishment of wrong, reluctantly and as a last resort if arbitration were impossible. These ideas had a long ancestry, but they were developed afresh from the standpoint of a

103 Benedictus de Spinoza:
contemporary anonymous portrait.

Dutchman writing amid the early crises of the Thirty Years' War and
shortly after the resumption of war with Spain in 1621. In the same
way Grotius's later ecumenical aspirations (which, however, aroused
the disapproval of his old Remonstrant friends) were still the response
of a Dutchman, brought up in a society in which different faiths were
indulged; and his pioneering Biblical criticism made use of Semitic
scholarship through his friendship with Manasseh ben Israel back in
Amsterdam.

Spinoza was both a Jew, and a Jew expelled with curses from his
own Amsterdam synagogue for his heretical opinions. In most places
the position of such an individual would not have been enviable. In
Holland he was not only left unmolested but had many friends among
the regents, including de Witt, and he received money from some of
them, as well as from grinding and polishing lenses. His *Tractatus
theologico-politicus* (1670) which was perhaps the first book to consider
the Bible as the work of men, in addition to less obvious 'atheistical'
features. The work also included a section recognizing Spinoza's
debt to the enlightened rule of the regents for freedom of thought
(even though the book was cautiously published under a false name),

and repaying it by defending the actions recently taken by the States of Holland, contrary to the wishes of the zealots in the church, to damp down criticisms of the Cartesian school. Spinoza praised and defended the freedom of judgment from which he had benefited, and had to be restrained from defending de Witt's memory from insult after de Witt was lynched in 1672. Though his writings fell under an official ban, Spinoza's funeral was accompanied by six carriages, and a large number of well-to-do people, to his last resting-place near de Witt's. The quality of his unorthodox mind was recognized by some of his contemporaries, though it was ignored for a long time afterwards.

DUTCH ART

Art, unlike literature, knows no barriers of language. Its qualities are open to all who can see, and the merits of Dutch art are the more easily appreciated because of its preoccupation with ordinary, everyday things, painted with extreme naturalism and technical skill. This, it is often said, is the art of a 'bourgeois' society. This line of thought

104 Jacob de Gheyn's studies of a field mouse are characteristic of the precision of Dutch draughtsmanship.

105 *Vanitas*: allegory on the death of Admiral Tromp. The skull, candle and musical instrument serve to recall the transience and vanity of earthly life.

should not, however, be pressed too far. Dutch painters and their works were soon in demand in other countries besides the Netherlands; and by the middle of the eighteenth century Dutch canvases were found everywhere from English country houses to the palace of the Hermitage in St Petersburg. They could, in fact, appeal to the taste of aristocrats and despots as well as to that of 'bourgeois'. Sometimes, too, the very realism of paintings can be deceptive. 'Every bloom in every flower piece is a symbol,' Huizinga has remarked, 'and the subject of every still life has emblematic as well as a natural significance.' Flower pieces may contain blooms from different seasons; landscapes may be imaginary – they were nearly always composed in studios; the details of church architecture may be altered to suit the needs of composition; genre paintings may turn out to be on the themes of the senses, or the seasons, and may have a didactic purpose.

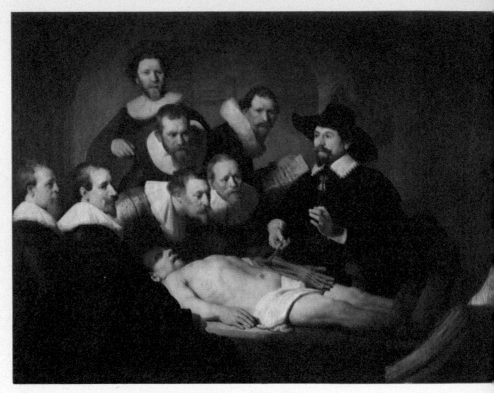

106 Rembrandt's *The Anatomy Lesson of Dr Tulp*.

Heckscher has argued at length that Rembrandt's *Anatomy of Dr Tulp* is anatomically incorrect, and deliberately so: that it alludes to the original derivation of the word *chirurgia*, and is concerned to portray Tulp as a second Vesalius. The apparently representational character of the paintings is subordinated to their purpose and to the needs of the composition.

What is beyond doubt is that the ownership of paintings in the Dutch Republic was far more widespread than in other countries, where they were the property of kings, nobles and churches. English visitors were startled by this. Early in the seventeenth century Dudley Carleton, passing through Leiden, 'noted as a singularity the common inn where we dined, which hath divers rooms hung with tapestry, and some furnished with pictures of the best hands.' Peter Mundy commented later on the general desire of people to adorn their houses, 'especially the outer or street room', with 'costly pieces'. Butchers and bakers had them in their shops, 'yea many times blacksmiths, cobblers, etc., will have some picture or other by their forge.' One may suspect some exaggerations here; on the other hand, Mundy makes no mention of prints, which were even cheaper and commoner than original paintings. Evelyn supplied a sophisticated explanation for the purchase of paintings by attributing it to the lack of opportunities for investment in land, as in England. This is a tempting idea but it is only a guess, unsupported by any evidence that people actually bought paintings for purposes of investment. There was

107 Vermeer's *The Love Letter* typifies the secular, everyday subjects of Dutch art.

after all no shortage of opportunity for commercial investment; if some concrete asset were desired it would have been more sensible to buy silver, and some of the people mentioned by Mundy could hardly have aspired to buy land anyway. It seems best to adopt the simple explanation that the Dutch delighted in looking at paintings (as they delighted in buying flowers), and were stimulated in this by the existence of a galaxy of talent to provide them.

The heights reached by the genius of the greatest of Dutch painters are remarkable, but the sheer number of artists of at least second-rank talent is no less so. The catalogue of Dutch paintings in the National Gallery in London includes works by some 160, all working within little more than a century. Precisely because there were so many artists, they were less well paid than their rivals in Flanders, France or Italy, and none of them achieved the status of a Rubens, van Dyck or Velazquez. They were craftsmen, and members of the St Lucas guild, along with glass-painters, bookbinders and so on. The prices that they could command were often not high. Group portraits were charged for in proportion to the number of figures in them. Hals's militiamen cost about 66 guilders each, Rembrandt's, in the so-called *Night Watch*, about 100. Ter Borch tried to sell his small painting of the Treaty of Münster, which included portraits of some fifty plenipotentiaries, for 6,000 guilders, but failed to do so. Lesser artists obtained much smaller rewards: Sir William Brereton, passing through Amsterdam in 1634, bought ten pictures for 64 guilders to take home to Cheshire. It is well known that some painters found it prudent to combine their art with some other occupation, and that others died in comparative poverty. Sometimes, however, as in Rembrandt's case, their plight has been misrepresented to some extent, in the interests of an argument about the neglect of artists by middle-class society. There is some evidence, from self-portraits and other sources, that the status of the successful artist was notably higher at the end of the seventeenth century than at the beginning.

In spite of the number of would-be purchasers, there was, in strictly economic terms, some 'over-production' of paintings. Many of these were commissioned, including the portraits which poured out in such profusion – Mierevelt's studio is said to have produced more than 5,000 portraits. Of other types of painting it is impossible to say how many were commissioned and how many were produced by the artist and then sold. It is certain that there were too many artists for them to be able to rely on the patronage of a few magnates, even if there had been more aristocrats in the United Provinces than there actually were; and patronage from the church came to a sudden end. That many painters were seeking to appeal to a wider public was an invitation to them to launch out on a wide variety of new subjects, and to specialize in those lines which were successful. Most of these were small easel-paintings, suitable for display on the walls of a comparatively small house. Some artists tended to paint marine pictures, with careful attention to the detailed rigging of the ships as well as to the moods of sea and sky, others interiors, genre pictures, scenes on the ice, 'flower-pieces' or views of the Dutch towns. The very words 'landscape' and 'still-life' have entered the English language from the Dutch; they were substantially Dutch inventions, just as genre painting is associated in most people's minds with the Netherlands.

Most of these subjects were secular ones. There seems to have been little demand for scenes from the lives of saints and martyrs, or for the medieval type of religious painting, even though there were Catholics among the artists as well as among the Dutch public: such pictures would have been less suitable for the home than as altar-pieces for which there was clearly no scope in the new religious scheme of things. Rembrandt and others produced religious pictures of a different type – and, still more, prints such as the 'Hundred Guilder' print – for a different sort of devotional use. Similarly, portraits were very rarely equestrian until the time of William III, and comparatively few of them were even full length. When Frederick Henry's widow, Amalia von Solms, wanted something large and grandiose to decorate the Oranjezaal in the Huis ten Bos in her husband's memory, she sent to Antwerp for Jordaens. The only large portraits were those of the groups of *schutterij*, such as Hals painted in Haarlem and Rembrandt in the *Night Watch*: these would be hung on the walls of the *doelen*, whereas those of individual sitters were intended for the more intimate surroundings of a house.

The increased number of paintings, the variety of new and secular subjects and the tendency of some artists to specialize in their own line were all features differentiating Dutch art from any that had preceded it. They carried with them a preoccupation with accurate draughtsmanship, and a devotion to the rendering of every detail with complete naturalism, however that detail might be used. A liking for realism had of course existed in Flemish art before the Revolt – it

108 Adam van Breen, *A Scene on the Ice*, one of the winter scenes popular with the Dutch public.

would be absurd to pretend that the Revolt marked a clean break with
everything that had gone before – but in this new and highly competitive situation, artists vied with one another to reproduce the exact
texture of cloth, the precise tone of flesh, the vivid trick of light, until
some, like Hoogstraten, indulged in deliberate *trompe-l'œil* to take in
the beholder. Some, like Hals, adopted more impressionistic techniques than others; but, in general, the purchaser clearly expected to
see reproduced on the canvas the details that he would see in his own
observation. In this, as in its variety, it is art for a large public rather
than for a sophisticated élite. The result is that Dutch art reproduces
probably more completely than any other the world in which painter
and client lived.

It is difficult to generalize about such a vast school of painters, but
to one observer at least the overriding impression is one of serenity,
of a secure world in which the observation of a moment could be

109 The naturalistic landscape:
Meindert Hobbema,
A Wooded Landscape with Cottages.

recollected in tranquillity and transferred to canvas for all time. With few exceptions the paintings are not restless and dynamic, are not concerned with political or religious controversy, and are without any really profound didactic purpose. Few are disturbing. There is little bitterness, nor are the religious paintings and the portraits of political figures strongly propagandist. Their world is one of order, decorum and stability, in which the possession of a painting adds to the comfortable pleasure of the owner of the house.

Engravings, however, were a different matter. There was so much interest in news, domestic and foreign, that there was a ready sale for prints, both satirical and descriptive. The bloodier events of Dutch history, like the execution of Oldenbarnevelt, the murder and mutilation of the brothers de Witt, or the atrocities of Spanish and French troops, were all commemorated; and the satires were so numerous as to cause offence to foreign monarchs. In 1663, for instance, Pepys remarked with mingled amusement and patriotic disapproval: 'I have been told two or three times, but today for certain I am told how in Holland publicly they have pictured our King with reproach. One way is with his pockets turned the wrong side outward, hanging out empty; another with two courtiers picking of his pockets; and a third leading of two ladies, while others abuse him; which amounts to great contempt.' The appeal of such cheap prints was to a very different side of the Dutch character from that of most of the paintings.

Most of the other arts in which the Dutch were interested again concerned objects which, like the paintings, gave aesthetic pleasure in the home: beautiful silverware; glass, including the special diamond-engraved variety on which the *précieuses* of the literary circle known as the Muidenkring laboured; and by 1640 tiles had become typical of Dutch interiors. Of more general European significance was the importation by the Dutch of Chinese porcelain, which was stimulated by the capture of about 100,000 pieces in a Portuguese ship, the *Caterina*, in 1604. There was a great auction at Amsterdam, and it was not long before many well-to-do people aspired to have their porcelain cupboard and a taste for 'china' spread to other countries. The first Dutch imitations were not very good, but by the last quarter of the seventeenth century factories at Delft were producing better and better Delftware. Apparently the decline of the breweries of Delft made buildings available just when demand developed for the new pottery.

110 Flemish pomp: Amalia von Solms commissioned the Antwerp painter Jacob Jordaens, rather than a native artist, to celebrate her husband's memory.

111 Detail of Samuel van Hoogstraten's perspective box, a startling example of Dutch artists' interest in *trompe l'œil*: the inside depicts two interiors, to be viewed from the peep-holes at each end.

In sculpture and in large-scale architecture, however, the Dutch did not excel. Their religion left no room for commissions of ecclesiastical sculpture; and there were no monarchs with palaces, and squares in front of them, to adorn. The most striking creations were monuments to national heroes, such as the tomb of William the Silent which stands

112, 113 The skill of Dutch craftsmen is displayed in this engraved glass goblet and silver ewer (below).

114 Tile picture of oriental flowers and birds.

116 The four continents pay homage to Amsterdam: west pediment of Amsterdam Town Hall.

where once the high altar stood, in the Nieuwe Kerk at Delft, and the nearby monument to the elder Tromp, with reliefs of naval battles which aroused Pepys's admiration when he saw them. But these were exceptional monuments to exceptional people. Neither the Calvinist religion nor the Dutch social structure encouraged the filling of churches with elaborate funeral monuments of the kind that appealed to the English gentry in Jacobean times. Outside in the market-places there were no equestrian statues of princes; indeed it has been said that a bronze statue of Erasmus at Rotterdam was the only public statue produced under the Republic. When sculptors were needed to produce allegorical decorations for the new Amsterdam Town Hall, the city fathers had to send for the Catholic Artus Quellin from Antwerp. It is said that he had to be restrained from including a bust of St Ignatius Loyola in his proposals.

It is significant that the grandest and most remarkable of the buildings erected in the Republic during the seventeenth century was neither a royal palace nor the equivalent of Hatfield House or Blenheim, but the new Town Hall of the city of Amsterdam, begun in 1648. In 1808 it became a royal palace, and it still stands as such on the Dam, in the heart of the city which was the strongest of the opponents of the House of Orange in the seventeenth century; but the symbolism of its decorations, inside and out, still indicates its original purpose. On its pediment the sea-gods and creatures from every continent gather to do homage to a figure representing Amsterdam. The contrast

115 Silver filigree clock of the late seventeenth century.

117, 118 Pieter Saenredam, *The Old Town Hall*, and (below) van der Heyden's *The New Town Hall*.

119 The Mauritshuis marked a new emphasis on classicism in Dutch architectural style.

between the old town hall, painted by Saenredam, and the new one depicted by van der Heyden, is extreme. Jacob van Campen was the architect who in Constantijn Huygens's words, 'From our stricken and disfigured face, The Gothic squint and squalor did erase.' He did this in a building which in its monumental style and wealth of decoration stood out from anything else in the city: it shows a taste quite different from that of the restrained elegance of the houses which were being built in the same period on the new *grachten*, no doubt for members of the same regent families, or even from the moderate classicism of the Mauritshuis, which had been built a little earlier at The Hague for Johan Maurits 'the Brazilian', who, between 1637 and 1644, had been Governor-General of Brazil. The same taste – not that which we associate with Dutch painting – showed itself when the burgomasters overruled the Calvinist Tulp's protest against the appearance of gods and goddesses on the triumphal cars during a state visit of the Prince of Orange in 1660. There was, after all, a place for a type of baroque in the service of authority in the Netherlands of the seventeenth century.

For most people, however, the brick houses reproduced in the paintings of Pieter de Hooch and Vermeer, or still to be seen on the old canal sides, are more characteristic of Dutch building, though it has to be recognized that these were often the houses of the more well-to-do sections of the population, and that many others continued to live in cottages of wood, particularly in the country. As has been seen, the late sixteenth and early seventeenth centuries saw a great increase in the size of the Dutch towns, particularly Amsterdam. Since oak beams were much less easily available than in England, half-timbered fronts were not reproduced: on the other hand, stone would have to be imported and was very costly. Brick was therefore the material commonly used. Often, too, circumstances dictated that all those who wanted a place on the canals could only be accommodated if they accepted a narrow frontage with the house extending back from it; there could be no question of a series of detached houses in the space available.

The result was the lines of houses whose tall, narrow façades with their *gevels* are the only feature seen by the passer-by. The ridged roofs were placed at right angles to the façade, which was not an essential

120 Frans Banningh Cocq's house in Amsterdam, with characteristic façade and *gevel*.

121 Berckheyde's painting of the newly built Herengracht gives a realistic contemporary impression of the elegance afforded by Amsterdam's town-planning.

part of the structure and might even be added after the roof had been put on the house proper. The *gevel* was almost the only form of external decoration which was possible, and as time passed new and less simple types of it were created. Many had pulleys attached to the end of the roof-beam so that heavy goods could be lifted into an attic or furniture moved in through the windows. The fact that so many of these houses survive in the modern Netherlands is a tribute to the solidity of their construction.

In front of the houses on each side of the canals there was often a cobbled street, no more than 20 feet wide, planted with trees. The canals themselves were often straightened, widened and deepened in the seventeenth century, and the old wooden bridges were replaced by stone ones.

In Amsterdam all this was regulated by a most remarkable scheme of town planning. Early in the seventeenth century the city council adopted its scheme for building along the three new concentric canals, the Herengracht, Keizersgracht and Prinsengracht. Along them would be town houses for merchants, while the lower middle class and artisans lived on radial canals. The council exercised powers of compulsory purchase (some councillors profiting from the scheme), and the land was divided into plots with a frontage averaging 26 feet and a depth averaging 180 feet. Since there was to be a minimum of 160 feet between the backs of buildings there was room for a garden of some 80 feet. Purchasers had to bind themselves not to use the premises for certain industrial purposes, and to use specified types of brick for the outside walls. The piling foundations had to be approved by municipal inspectors before building could begin. Eventually the new owners had to pay, in proportion to their frontage, for the making of the streets and the provision of stone retaining walls for the canals. The council itself built almost nothing, but within the conditions it laid down the result was remarkably homogeneous and attractive, as any tourist can still observe if he is willing to avoid the traffic and the parked cars. The Jordaan in the west was developed by speculators to provide cheaper and more crowded houses for immigrant workpeople.

The houses on the *grachten* had comparatively small rooms; they needed relatively few servants and were easy for housewives with no other occupation to keep clean, particularly as water was abundant for use on the tiled floors. The Dutch preoccupation with cleanliness was something that foreigners like Temple could not understand. Even the streets in front of the houses (said a French visitor) were kept so clean that foreigners had scruples about spitting on them. The *huisvrouw* wanted her home to be *schoon* in both senses of the Dutch word, clean as well as beautiful, and she might be as proud of the white linen in her linen cupboard as of the objects that her husband collected to ornament the place.

Sometimes, no doubt, this preoccupation with cleanliness was carried to excess, and the Dutch told stories against themselves about it, 'and some so extravagant', said Temple,

> that my sister took them for jest; when the Secretary of Amsterdam, that was of the company, desiring her to look out of the window, said, Why, Madam, there is the House where one of our magistrates going to visit the mistress of it, and knocking at the door, a strapping North Holland lass came and opened it; he asked, whether her mistress was at home, she said, yes; and with that he offered to go in: but the wench marking his shoes were not very clean, took him by both arms, threw him upon her back, carried him across two rooms, set him down at the bottom of the stairs, pulled off his shoes, put him on a pair of slippers that stood there, all this without saying a word; but when she had done, told him, he might go up to her mistress, who was in her chamber.

But their 'house-pride', like their style of domestic architecture, fitted in with man's growing desire for privacy in the early modern period and encouraged a new domestic intimacy. It was in this setting that many of the Dutch paintings were intended to be hung.

DUTCH SCIENCE

Dutch scientists, like Dutch artists, were intent on observing and recording new features of the world around them; and just as Dutch art was secular in so many of its subjects, so too the effect of the work of many of the scientists was to contribute to the secularization of thought. 'Wonder is no wonder' was the motto of Simon Stevin.

122 Cleanliness and order predominate in a characteristic Dutch interior: Pieter de Hooch's *Interior with Mother and Child*.

The work of Stevin, and of many other Dutch scientists, was strongly utilitarian, rather than theoretical, in its attitudes. It took into account the urgent practical needs of the day: it tended to be 'applied' rather than 'pure'. Stevin himself was patronized by Prince Maurice, who founded for him a school of engineering at Leiden (where he lectured, not in Latin but in Dutch), and made use of his services in the new scientific methods of warfare which he employed. The book translated into English as *The Havenfinding Art* aimed at providing practical solutions to the problems of navigation faced by Dutch sailors on their world-wide voyages, in days when there was no satisfactory way of calculating longitude. His book, *De Thiende* (1585), translated in 1608 as *Disme: the Art of Tenths, or Decimal Arithmetike*, was not the first to advocate a 'decimal system', but it did a great deal to demonstrate its superiority over common fractions. The relevance of another treatise on double-entry book-keeping to the needs of a mercantile nation needs no emphasis.

123, 124 Simon Stevin, the mathematician, and (right) title-page of the first English edition of his *De Thiende*.

DISME:
The Art of Tenths,
OR,
Decimall Arithmetike,

Teaching how to performe all Computations whatsoeuer, by whole Numbers without Fractions; by the foure Principles of Common Arithmeticke: namely, Addition, Substraction, Multiplication, and Diuision.

Inuented by the excellent Mathematician, Simon Steuin.

Published in English with some additions by Robert Norton, Gent.

Imprinted at London by *S. S.* for *Hugh Astley*, and are to be sold at his shop at Saint Magnus corner. 1608.

125, 126 Left: the reverse side of an original pendulum clock of 1657 using Christian Huygens's pendulum mechanism; the front view displays the maker's name.

Willibrord Snellius, Professor of Mathematics at Leiden, whose observatory has already been referred to, was responsible for developing methods of triangulation. The Botanical Garden at Leiden was intended for severely practical purposes – originally for the growth of medicinal herbs for the training of medical students – though the interests which it indirectly fostered included the absurd wave of financial speculation on the tulip. In the 1650s Christian Huygens, the greatest of the Dutch scientists, developed pendulum clocks which were intended to solve the same problem of navigation that had confronted Stevin. His clocks and his watches with their spiral balances were more accurate than any previously known, though their lack of a compensating mechanism meant that they were still not accurate enough under all conditions to achieve their main aim.

Perhaps the most striking discoveries, however, were made with the aid of the lens, whether in the telescope or the microscope. Whoever first invented these instruments, the Dutch made better lenses than anyone else, and with their aid saw things which had not previously been seen by any human eye. Through the telescope Huygens observed the ring and moons of Saturn; through the microscope Leeuwenhoek was the first man to see protozoa in rainwater, and bacteria in the human mouth and excrement, and to observe spermatozoa.

Leeuwenhoek was not the inventor of the microscope – Petrus Borellus published the first book of microscopic observations in 1656 – and some of the theories of reproduction which he erected on the basis of his observations proved to be incorrect; but the observations themselves, made with a simple lens, were remarkable. In his enthusiasm he even tried to watch an explosion of gunpowder under a microscope and nearly blinded himself, but he survived to have the quality of his work as a microscopist recognized by his election to a Fellowship of the Royal Society in London. Jan Swammerdam was interested in insects – dragonflies, ants, bees, butterflies, locusts and spiders. He observed for the first time the pairing of the dragonfly and studied its life-cycle, investigated the spider's web, built an artificial ants' nest to make his examination of them easier, and discussed the anatomy of the bee and established the sex of the queen. 'The Omnipotent Finger of God', he wrote, 'is here presented in the anatomy of the Louse, in which you will find wonder heaped upon wonder, and will be amazed at the Wisdom of God manifest in a most minute matter.' For such men as these there was, after all, a kind of wonder, though it was very different from the supernatural interventions in which men had formerly believed.

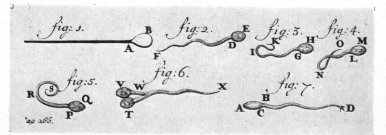

127 Spermatozoa as seen by Leeuwenhoek: figures 1 and 7 are from man, the rest from sheep.

128 Microscope made by Leeuwenhoek.

129 Scientific instruments decorate the frontispiece of Jan Swammerdam's *De Respiratione.* ▶

Except for Maurice's encouragement of Stevin, all these individuals made their scientific discoveries without patronage from political and ecclesiastical authorities – and without serious interference from them. There was nothing like the French Académie des Sciences, to which Huygens migrated, and the great Leeuwenhoek, since he spoke no Latin, was not even promoted to a university chair. On the other hand, there was no prosecution like that of Galileo, not because conservative theologians, such as Voetius, did not inveigh against the new cosmography, but because they had no sanctions at their disposal. In this respect, as in others, the loose structure of the Republic favoured intellectual freedom.

THE POOR

A civilization must be judged not simply on its political, economic, intellectual and artistic achievements, but on the quality of life which it affords to the poor and the less fortunate members of society. If humanitarian criteria are applied to the Dutch people in the seventeenth century, how well do they stand up to close examination?

In some ways the lot of the ordinary Dutchman was better than that of his neighbours. His was a relatively peaceful existence, even though his country was at war for the best part of a century. From the mid-1590s most Dutch territory was free from devastation by invading forces. Even the brief crisis of 1672–73, when Louis XIV established himself in the centre of the United Provinces at Utrecht, was not at all comparable with the campaigns of the Thirty Years' War, Louis XIV's invasions of the Palatinate or Marlborough's campaign in Bavaria. Again, the internal problems of the Union were settled without civil war. There was nothing like the rebellions in England and Ireland, the campaigns against the Huguenots, the Frondes and the revolt of the Camisards in France, the revolts of Catalans and Portuguese against Castile, the 'Time of the Troubles' or the rising of Stenka Razin in Russia. The Dutchman neither suffered from the depredations of armies nor was compelled to enlist in them. Even *banditti* and highwaymen did not present a very serious problem. The Republic was an oasis of order and peace in a troubled century. This in itself was no small blessing, and the enlightened policies of the Republic's rulers deserve some of the credit for it.

The Dutchman also seems to have been better fed, or at any rate less badly fed, than most of his contemporaries. He was less subject to the bad weather, bad harvests and famine which drove the French peasants to the brink of starvation, or over it, in bad years. There is a paradox here, too, for even in the best years the Dutch could not grow enough food themselves and had to supplement their crops by imports of grain from the Baltic; but this was so well organized and distributed through Amsterdam that, however much others further afield might suffer, the Dutch did not starve. The danger was that a northern war might block the Sound, as it had done in the troubled years of the 1560s, but Dutch policy was on its guard against this. It has even been suggested that through a relative abundance of meat, fish and cheese there was more protein in the Dutchman's diet than in that of other people, though it seems unlikely that the lower classes ate meat very often.

To plague, on the other hand, the seaports were particularly vulnerable, and there were serious epidemics in Amsterdam and elsewhere,

130 Jan Steen's *The Lean Kitchen*: a rare portrayal of the sufferings of the poor rather than the comfort of the wealthy.

though none with as many victims as the Great Plague of 1665 in London. Possibly the number of modern brick houses reduced the danger; possibly those attacked were less weakened by malnutrition. As always the poorer classes suffered most, and in the conditions of the day the authorities were powerless to do very much about it.

If war, famine and epidemic were the three greatest evils which most Europeans had to face, the fourth was certainly taxation. Contemporaries were in no doubt that the Dutch were very heavily taxed: they remarked that the demands were very much heavier than Alva's *alcabala* against which the provinces had originally protested, and marvelled that the Dutch accepted their burden without complaint. With a population only a third as large as that of England, they paid more in ordinary taxation than the English did to Charles II. If the Dutch avoided some of the other disadvantages of war, they did not escape the cost of maintaining an army and navy. And though there was a 'hundredth penny' on estates, chimney money and a stamp tax, a heavy proportion was raised by indirect taxation which, as always, weighed more heavily on the poor than on the rich. It was from the Dutch that other countries caught the habit of imposing excises. There was an astonishing variety of these. Temple remarked that, 'when in a tavern, a certain dish of fish is eaten with the usual sauce, above thirty several excises are paid.' English visitors found this variety of taxes on consumption so remarkable that they sometimes overlooked that customs duties were low, and that no tithes were payable to the church. Riots against some of the excises were not unknown, but there was nothing of the scale, the desperation or the frequency of the French risings under Louis XIII. And the general level of prosperity was such that there was little emigration to Dutch colonies like New Amsterdam, and much immigration into the Dutch cities from other countries.

Poverty was therefore not as grinding as in some other places, but it was severe enough, and indeed was made worse by the commercial

131 Peasants, fishermen and townspeople look out to sea, the source of Dutch prosperity.

and industrial nature of the Dutch economy, which meant that employment fluctuated. There was much seasonal unemployment for sailors, fishermen and those working in ancillary industries, quite apart from periods of special depression. So much commercial activity was speculative that there were bound to be booms and slumps, sometimes influenced by the international situation. Conditions were probably even worse in Leiden than in the seaports. The city was heavily dependent on the textile industry, and, though production continued to increase until 1671, expansion was not always steady, and it was only won by means of low real wages, bad housing and poor conditions. The extent of the poverty which resulted is difficult to measure. In 1622 some 10,000 of the people of Leiden were excused payment of a poll-tax for reasons of poverty. In 1688 the English consul at Amsterdam, William Carr, wrote that the city was said to have 20,000 poor every day at bed and board, but this and other similar estimates can only be guesses. In any case, there is no means of knowing whether high figures result from greater poverty or greater generosity than elsewhere: definitions of poverty vary from place to place and from time to time.

It is certain that the Dutch were much preoccupied with the problem of the poor. It did not lead them to devise schemes for greater social justice – the unquestioned assumption was that the poor would always be with them, and that their condition had to be alleviated by the philanthropic efforts of Christians. There was a long tradition of charitable endowments in the civic communities of the Netherlands, dating back well before the Reformation. At the time of the Revolt all church and monastic property was seized by the city authorities, but a far greater proportion of the confiscated wealth than in England was devoted to educational and charitable purposes – so much so that this has been given as one reason for the Protestantization of the poor. But the efforts of the burghers, whether 'libertine' or orthodox Calvinists, did not stop there. As the cities grew they provided money, almshouses

(in pleasant-looking brick *hofjes,* many of them still to be seen), and regents to govern them. Calvinists might not believe in the efficacy of good works to earn salvation, but they accepted an obligation to do God's work in the world by relieving poverty. Calvin had created his deacons, and nowhere were their duties taken more seriously than in the congregations of the Dutch Republic.

No doubt some of the charity which resulted was rather cold. Hals's portrait of the women governors of an almshouse at Haarlem, painted when he was over eighty, is terrifying in its brilliance. Some allowance must be made for the bitterness of an old man who had himself been reduced to the position of an inmate of such an almshouse, but it is easy to imagine that some of the respectable people who took it upon themselves to govern did so for social reasons rather than from warmth of heart. As always, the motives of some who gave must have been mixed. There is a legend that the great entrepreneur and armaments dealer, de Geer, who did so much to develop the copper and iron resources of Sweden and eventually entered the Swedish nobility, never insured his ships, but if they arrived safely, gave the equivalent of the premium to the poor, so that it was profitable to God to look after his business interests. But this may be unfair to the generosity which de Geer, a pious Calvinist, displayed throughout his life. It is too easy to be cynical about other people's motives; it is better to abstain from trying to sit in judgment on the givers, and to fall back on the simple fact that the provision made for the poor, the insane and the orphans excited the admiration of every foreign visitor.

William Carr often had occasion to be contemptuous about the Dutch, but was unstinting in his praise of

> the acts of charity of Amsterdam, the which is so extraordinary that they surpass all other cities in the world, for they are daily and hourly giving to the poor. Every house in Amsterdam hath a box hanging in a chain on which is written *Think on the poor,* so that, when any merchant sells goods they commonly conclude no bargain, but more or less is put in the poor's box; these boxes are locked up by the Deacons, who once a quarter go round the city and take the money out of the boxes. Then twice a week there are men belonging to the hospitals [almshouses] that go round the city and ring a bell at every house to know what the master or mistress of the house will give to the box, who generally give not less than

132 The old people's home, Amsterdam, with its attractive gardens.

2 stivers. Then every first Wednesday of the month the Deacons in their turn go round the city from house to house to receive what every house keeper will give to the poor. Then on the week before the sacrament is given, a minister with an elder goes round the city to every house where any members of the Protestant religion live, and there ask if any differences be in the family, offering their service to reconcile them . . . at this time . . . the people take an occasion to give to the poor. . . .

He went on to quote the King of England as saying, at the time of the French invasion in 1672, 'that he was of opinion that God would preserve Amsterdam from being destroyed if it were only for the great charity they have for the poor.' Actors were made to pay a substantial contribution, and 'that sort of unnecessary vermin which frequent fairs' paid every third penny of the money that they took at their booths.

133 Frans Hals, *The Women Governors of the Old Men's Home.*

The deacons of Amsterdam had an income and expenditure of 100,000 florins in 1617, which was trebled by the end of the century, and this was only part of what was spent on charitable purposes. It is likely that members of the Calvinist church were in a more favourable position than others, just as more was available for the lower classes in the cities than for the rural poor; but to a certain extent every part of the community and every congregation was under pressure to try to conform to a generally high standard. James Howell, who commented that it was as rare to see a beggar in Amsterdam as to see a horse in Venice, was exaggerating – that there were beggars is clear from the drawings of some of the artists – but he was implicitly making a valid comparison with the numbers of beggars and vagrants in England.

Visitors to Amsterdam were taken to see the almshouses for the old ('more like princes' palaces than lodgings for poor people', said Carr) and the orphanages for the young – the children of citizens and of strangers, as well as foundlings. There were some hundreds of boys and girls living there, taught to read and write and trained for some work, and, according to Carr, 'held in such veneration and respect that a man had as good strike a burgomaster's child as one of them.' The discipline must have been fairly strict, and one suspects that sometimes when the children had grown up they were a cheap source of labour, but they were better off than the children of many other capital cities. The *Dolhuis* for the care of the insane was also compared favourably with the London Bedlam – 'it is so stately, that one would take it to be the house of some lord', wrote Marmaduke Rawdon. Evelyn kept his greatest admiration for the Amsterdam 'hospital for their lame and decrepit soldiers, it being for state, order and accommodations one of the worthiest things that I think the world can show of that nature.' It had been founded in 1587; Chelsea Hospital was established in 1682. Temple admired a similar home for aged seamen at Enkhuizen.

Seventeenth-century tourists also visited the *Rasphuis*. This too was much admired, and there was even a German imitation of it, but it represents a sterner side of the Dutch character. It was a house of correction for petty thieves, those guilty of minor crimes of violence, cheats and confidence tricksters, who were compelled to rasp a set amount of hard brazilwood each week, for use in dyeing. The *Spinhuis* was a house of correction for women – harlots, drunks and scolds.

134 A contemporary print pictures the *Rasphuis*.

135 Entrance of the Amsterdam bankruptcy office: the frieze above the lintel represents the fall of Icarus, and the relief shows torn money-bags, an empty money-box and a bundle of unpaid bills.

Torture was used on criminals, the more because the city authorities had no power to pronounce a death sentence unless the prisoner had first confessed his guilt. Death sentences may have been frequent, to judge from Constantijn Huygens's observation of fifty gibbets within 120 miles. This was the blackest side of life in the United Provinces; the enlightenment of the regents did not extend to the treatment of crime, except to the extent that people from different classes were treated alike. A Frenchman was surprised to find a member of a noble family executed for killing a member of the watch at The Hague: in France and England such a crime would have been pardoned. This was the same egalitarian spirit in which the exiled King of Bohemia, hunting across standing crops in the fashion to which he was accustomed, found himself assailed by a peasant with a pitchfork. Noble birth conferred little privilege, at least in the west of the country. But it might be imprudent for someone from the lower classes to bring a civil action against a regent: he could do so, but his chances might not be good.

There were two features of the civil law of Holland which won the admiration of Englishmen. One was the provision of arbitrators who would try to reconcile the parties before action was actually engaged in court. Hugh Peters, who exercised a ministry in Rotterdam before he went home to be present at Charles I's execution and become one of the Rump's commission for legal reform, found this one of the features of Dutch society that he could commend. Secondly, there was the speedy and efficient settlement of cases of debt by commissioners for that purpose in the town hall. For both creditors and debtors the system was much more convenient than the dilatory and cumbersome one in England against which some of the radicals protested in the middle years of the century: creditors found it easier and quicker to get satisfaction and debtors did not languish aimlessly in prison. This was one of the many ways in which the interests of commerce could be fostered by the authorities. Others were the Amsterdam postal service, municipal improvements such as

136 3S (3 stuiver) was postage due on this early example of a letter sent through the Amsterdam mail.

137 The new fire-hose explained: the older model (left) reached only as far as the outside wall; the new type could be extended inside.

the introduction of street lighting and the invention of a fire-hose (in both of which the painter Jan van der Heyden was concerned), and the regular service of boats which linked Amsterdam with Leiden, Delft and Rotterdam along the inland waterways at scheduled times. These were not matters to be left by the authorities to private enterprise.

Inevitably there was much in life that was hard, disagreeable and dangerous, even in this relatively prosperous and peaceful part of Europe; but there were also recreations. The more stern and extreme Calvinist theologians like Voetius of Utrecht might thunder against many popular amusements, but it was, one often feels, more to mark their disapproval than because they seriously expected the authorities to take action against them. The regents would not contemplate allowing the church to be as rigorous as in Geneva. Most Saint's days were abolished but Saint Nicholas continued to call on 6 December, bringing with him Black Peter – from Spain. There were plenty of Jan Steen households. The *kermesses* were still held in every town and village, usually lasting a week, but sometimes two and occasionally three: William III, unlikely as it might seem, was particularly fond of the one at The Hague, where even princes and magistrates might mingle with the crowd. In winter there was skating and sport on the ice. Music did not disappear under any alleged Calvinist blight: the painters show us both the singing of the low-life revellers and the music lessons for the well-to-do. For all, there were at some time the pleasures of food, drink and tobacco, though Maurice tried to prohibit smoking in the army and Piet Hein in his fleet. Calvinists, too,

138 Revelling and carousing: Jan Steen's *Merry Company*, 1666–70.

139, 140 Entertainment and relaxation: *Coster's Nederduitsche Academie*, the first theatre in Amsterdam, and (below) children's sports.

enjoyed these pleasures: Tulp's meal on the occasion of his jubilee lasted from 2 to 11 p.m.

Finally, a few words about the depressed classes of women, children and servants. All of these were thought by foreigners to have more freedom than elsewhere – indeed, too much of it. Fynes Moryson was astonished to hear the town crier summoning a man before the magistrate for beating his wife. He went further:

> By the foresaid privilege of wives to dispose goods by their last will, and by the contracts in respect of their dowry (which to the same end use to be warily drawn), they keep their husbands in a kind of awe, and almost alone, without their husbands inter-meddling, not only keep their shops at home, but exercise traffic abroad. Nothing is more frequent, than for little girls to insult over their brothers much bigger than they, reproving their doings, and calling them great lubbers, whereof when I talked with some scholars my companions, as a fashion seeming strange to me, they were so far from wondering thereat, as they told me, it was a common thing for wives to drive their husbands and their friends out of the doors with scolding, as if they consumed the goods wherein they had a property with their husbands.

His picture of 'this unnatural domineering over their husbands' is obviously overdrawn, but comments of this sort are sufficiently common to make one believe that some wives were more partners in the household than subjects, as they might be elsewhere. The Frenchman Jean de Parival, who remarked on this, also criticized the Dutch for being too indulgent to their children and not beating them sufficiently; but perhaps his greatest complaint was that the maid-servants were so privileged that even their masters dared not strike them. If someone got into a rage and beat his maid or turned her out *par quelque rudesse*, he was liable to pay a fine and the girl's wages in full, 'even if they were not due and she deserved it.' 'The cloth', said Moryson, 'is laid four times in the day for very servants, but two of these times they set before them nothing but cheese and butter.' Many in other countries could not say as much. It is striking how often maidservants, children and pet dogs are portrayed in the paintings of the period.

'Bene qui latuit, bene vixit', said Descartes, quoting Ovid. There were many people living in the United Provinces besides Descartes (who spent thirty years there) who preferred conditions there to those in the country of their birth; and many of them were fugitives for political or religious reasons.

When Pierre Bayle described the Republic as 'the great ark of the refugees', he was not thinking only of the wave of Huguenot exiles of whom he was one. The phrase occurs in one of his biographical articles on a sixteenth-century scholar. The Huguenots who came to Amsterdam after the Revocation of the Edict of Nantes were only the latest of a series of immigrants over more than a century, and the reception the Dutch gave to these fugitives, scholars and others, was one of their greatest contributions to European civilization.

We have previously mentioned the first great wave of immigrants who came north from Flanders and Brabant to seek greater religious and political freedom or greater economic opportunity. Those who were Dutch-speaking were readily absorbed into the Dutch people and their churches, acting in many cases as an invigorating influence upon them. The French-speaking or Walloon element, however, preserved some identity much longer: they were slow to learn Dutch, and preferred to worship in their own Walloon churches. These were fully recognized by the Calvinist church authorities and affiliated to their *classes*. In time, some of their members transferred, but they were joined by others, including some regent families. These churches tended to become 'fashionable', preaching a more liberal Calvinism and, like the Remonstrants, attracting scholars, contributing to intellectual life, and favourably regarded by the authorities.

Such a Walloon church is still to be seen in Leiden. Now a library, it stands near to the Pieterskerk, where lies buried (in addition to Scaliger, Boerhaave, Arminius and others) John Robinson, the pastor of the Pilgrim Fathers after their first departure from England. Close by, on the site where Robinson lived and taught, is now the Jan Pesijnshofje, an almshouse built in 1683 for Huguenots who had fled from the persecution of Louis XIV. The stones of the small square carry memories of more than one set of foreigners, who were welcomed, or at least tolerated in Leiden.

The story of the Pilgrim Fathers illustrates the way in which Dutch 'liberty' worked to the advantage of small unorthodox groups. In

1609 William Brewster, William Bradford and John Robinson, who had at first settled in Amsterdam, were induced by their quarrels and difficulties there to ask permission of the Leiden magistrates to move to the university city. A reply was forthcoming: '[We] refuse no honest persons ingress to come and have their residence in this city, provided that such persons behave themselves honestly, and submit to all the laws and ordinances here.' Later the magistrates stonewalled the protests of James I's ambassador. They struck no heroic attitudes, but simply recited Robinson's request and their reply. Later the exiles founded a printing-press whose productions were unwelcome to James I, and there were official complaints against them. The city magistrates were plainly far from eager to find those responsible, but it was awkward to risk forfeiting James's friendship. At the instance of the States of Holland they reluctantly agreed to summon Brewster and his patron, Thomas Brewer, before them. Brewster was probably allowed to escape; Brewer was arrested and his books and type seized by the university authorities (since he was enrolled at the university). James I requested his extradition, and a long process of stalling followed, with the Dutch pleading University privilege to the English ambassador. Eventually they let Brewer go to England, but in the company of a beadle, and on a promise that he would be permitted to return from London after examination. Even this action by the Dutch authorities was highly unusual, and perhaps only taken because this was the year of the Synod of Dort. Brewer returned safely and Brewster was never caught. This was one example out of many of the way in which pressures could be evaded by unwilling local authorities under the Dutch system of government.

Robinson and most of his group stayed behind in Leiden when the rest set out on their famous journey across the Atlantic. They were by no means the only dissenters from the Anglican church who preferred to worship in their own way in Holland. There was a succession of Separatists, Brownists, Baptists, Fifth Monarchy Men, and other sectaries, reaching their largest numbers in the period of Archbishop Laud. There were also, however, the 'English churches' (some of them including Scots as well as English Presbyterians) which were set up in Amsterdam, Leiden, Rotterdam, and other places. Like the Walloon churches, they worshipped in their own language and had their own consistory, but were part of the *classes* of the official Calvinist church: their ministers, like Dutch ones, required the

141 The English church in Amsterdam.

approval of the city magistrates before being admitted, and received a
salary from them – about £100 in the first half of the century. The
English church in the Begijnhof at Amsterdam still survives, having
held services continuously since the beginning of the seventeenth
century except for the years 1940–45. But the English churches did
not acquire the same social position as some of the Walloon ones,
partly because fewer of the regents could speak their language.

There were also more aristocratic, even royal refugees, who came
to the Netherlands for political reasons; but these were more commonly the guests of the House of Orange than private citizens under
the protection of municipalities. Frederick, Elector Palatine and King
of Bohemia, came with his wife Elizabeth, five sons and four daughters.
Charles I's Queen, Henrietta Maria, came to seek help from her
son-in-law and to try and pawn the royal jewels. Charles II was in
The Hague when he heard the news of his father's execution and came
back there before he sailed to recover his throne in 1660. Shaftesbury
went there to die in 1683. The Duke of Monmouth was banished
there at the end of Charles's reign, and later took advantage of the

looseness of the Dutch constitution to prepare his ships and sail away from Amsterdam to his ill-fated rebellion, in spite of the efforts of James II's ambassador to prevent him.

But princes and statesmen could usually find refuge in some friendly court or other. What was distinctive about the Republic was the indulgence it gave to humbler refugees with whom the regents did not sympathize, despite demands for their extradition. After the Restoration of 1660 there came regicides and other radicals, and the sailors who piloted de Ruyter's ships up the Medway; there were those who found England too hot to hold them after the Rye House Plot in 1683, and the scattered remnants of Monmouth's adventurers, hoping for better days. The handing-over of Sir Thomas Armstrong, to be taken back to England for execution, was one of the rare occasions on which foreign monarchs were successful in obtaining the extradition of wanted men. As a rule, English and French ambassadors, pressing for action to arrest rebels or pamphleteers, were constantly frustrated by the division of authority between stadholder, States-General, States of Holland, and city magistrates. *[margin note: bureaucracy at best]*

A different category was that of the scholar who settled in the Republic for the sake of its liberal atmosphere, without necessarily being proscribed by his own government. Notable among these was René Descartes, who was not driven out of France but who found it convenient to settle in Holland between 1620 and 1649 and to issue from a Dutch press his *Discours de la Méthode*. Whether it could have been published from a French press is doubtful; it would certainly not have received such currency. Descartes was not an unqualified admirer of the Dutch: like many French exiles, he did not trouble to learn the language, and had remarks to make about the ignoble Dutch concern with trade. But he was able to think and to write there, his Walloon acquaintances helped to circulate his ideas, and he made some important scholarly friends, including Comenius. The great Czech educationalist spent the last fourteen years of his life in the Netherlands after vainly seeking a resting-place elsewhere.

John Locke also came to the Republic, not officially pursued by Charles II's government, but knowing that he was at least looked upon with disfavour. His stay, from 1683 to 1689, was an extremely important period of his life. He had long been a believer in toleration, at least for Protestants, but his practical experience of it in the Dutch cities served to confirm his opinion that it would work. Like other exiles, he was not given an enthusiastic reception – he was little known as yet – but he was allowed to stay in Amsterdam, Utrecht and Rotterdam, living a retired, cautious and scholarly life. Once he was 'moved on' from Utrecht, but he was otherwise undisturbed. Some of his most important friendships were with men from the small Remonstrant group, now tacitly indulged, mild, liberal, rational and tolerant in their views. The two most important were Philip van Limborch and Jean Le Clerc, both professors at the Remonstrant Seminary in Amsterdam, but two very different types. Limborch was pastor, philosopher, and professor of theology; Le Clerc, born in Geneva of Huguenot parents, was responsible for one of the first scholarly reviews, the *Bibliothèque Universelle*, and he persuaded Locke for the first time to allow some of his views to appear in print. An abbreviated version of the *Essay Concerning Human Understanding* appeared in 1687, and for some months Locke reviewed most of the important new books there. The *Epistola de Tolerantia* was published at Gouda in 1689. Its insistence that Christianity cannot be imposed by force, and that the civil government had no business to compel conformity to any version of it, commended it to many Dutch readers.

Locke was able to witness the arrival in the Netherlands of the largest numbers of Huguenots ever. Before Louis XIV actually revoked the Edict of Nantes in 1685, conditions in France had been deteriorating for some time, and in 1681 the Huguenots appealed to the magistrates of the Dutch cities for help. In a public declaration the city of Amsterdam promised to grant refugees the freedom of the city, together with exemption from taxes for three years, advances for the purchase of the tools of their trade, and even an engagement to buy their products; and the States of Holland followed by freeing refugees from all taxes for twelve years. The Revocation speeded up the flight of the Huguenots, and in the following year the French ambassador's agent estimated that there were nearly 75,000 of them in the Republic. This large number, comparable with the total population of any Dutch city except Amsterdam, may be an overestimate; but they were certainly numerous enough to test the powers of any state to assimilate them. Some 250 pastors arrived, and to them the States of Holland allocated 25,000 florins for immediate relief, and later there were pensions for some of them (400 florins for married clergy, 200 for bachelors) and pastorates. In the year 1685 there were twenty-six Walloon churches; by 1688 there were sixty-two, all of them

142 Pierre Bayle, deprived of his chair in the *Illustre School* for his support of tolerance, nevertheless remained in the Republic, free to publish his famous *Dictionnaire*: an eighteenth-century portrait by Carl Vanloo.

supported from municipal funds. It would be wrong to suppose that the sudden arrival of these foreigners caused no difficulties; there were some local jealousies, and William III had to press for those who were soldiers to be taken into the army. Official attitudes were generally sympathetic – indeed the arrival of the Huguenots did much to reconcile Amsterdam to a policy of hostility towards Louis XIV, and the difficulties were smoothed over. Many of the Huguenots at first believed that their exile from France would only be temporary. When Burnet and many other English refugees from popish tyranny returned to their own country in 1688–89, they were confident that God would soon vindicate their cause too and bring about a reversal of fortune in France. It was not until after the Treaty of Rijswijk in 1697 that many of them accepted that their exile would be lifelong.

For a few of the scholars among the Huguenots the city authorities of Rotterdam decided to set up an *Illustre School*. Chairs in this were offered to both Pierre Bayle and Jean Jurieu, who had previously been colleagues and friends at the Huguenot Academy of Sedan. The school was supposed to have some of the characteristics of a university without the power to confer degrees, but it never developed very far. There was little prospect of competing with the well-known University of Leiden, with its much more numerous professoriate. It is likely that the main motive of those who set it up was to provide a means of relief for Bayle and others. His task as a professor was practically a sinecure, for he had little taste for lecturing and neither his public lectures nor his private classes were ever well attended; but he did enjoy a certain status, a modest income, and a considerable amount of leisure, in which he established his literary reputation with his *Nouvelles de la République des Lettres* between 1684 and 1687. The eventual loss of his chair needs to be seen against this background.

The person most responsible for the agitation against Bayle was his former friend Jurieu, and the basic reason for their disagreement was their differing views on the subject of toleration. Bayle, no doubt fortified by his observation of the loyalty of religious minorities to the Dutch state as long as they were allowed freedom of conscience, believed that force was against the general spirit of the Gospels, that an ideal society would extend its protection to all religions, and that, since most theological problems were incapable of proof, man should pray for those that he cannot convince, rather than oppress them. He thought (unlike Locke) that even atheism could be allowed to exist without fear of its undermining the foundations of society. But his commentary on Christ's words, 'Compel them to come in', published in Amsterdam in 1686, was attacked by Jurieu, who thought that it led straight to Deism and gave excessive rights to the individual conscience. Continuing the line of the more rigid Calvinists in the Republic, he believed that princes had a special duty to maintain the purity of the faith by using their authority to repress dissenting sects – not to the extent of the death penalty, but by means of discriminatory measures, including the deprivation of civic privileges. Jurieu regarded Bayle as a traitor in the holy war against Papist France, which his reading of the Apocalypse told him would soon end in success, and in his pamphlets he pressed accusations of Socinianism against Bayle with considerable violence. But he could achieve nothing except Bayle's dismissal from his chair, and even that was probably only because in 1693 there was a minor municipal *coup* in Rotterdam which put the allies of Bayle's enemies into power. On 30 October Bayle was deprived of his sinecure, officially on grounds of economy. But in practice he suffered hardly at all. He took a pension from the bookseller Leers, did not even have to leave Rotterdam, and himself spoke of 'le plus grand et le plus charmant loisir qu'un homme de lettres puisse souhaiter'. It has even been suggested that the loss of his chair was a piece of good luck which enabled him to devote himself entirely to his writing.

It was still in Rotterdam, therefore, that the volumes of Bayle's famous *Dictionnaire* appeared, not in his native country: not only was permission not given to reprint the first edition in France, but the mere entry of the book into France was forbidden. Again, this important book, which led to Bayle's being described as 'the father of scepticism', was not dedicated to any great aristocratic patron, as would probably have been the case in other societies. The only patron Bayle needed was his publisher, who in turn relied on the existence of a sufficiently large international reading public for a book which appeared from a Dutch printing-press: one more illustration of the link between the Republic as a great publishing centre and the relative freedom of thought which existed there. Bayle lived on until 1706, poor but enjoying considerable independence and quietly attending the Walloon church in spite of the accusations of Deism. Meanwhile his reputation grew and his ideas on toleration, if not his generally sceptical outlook, became more acceptable than Jurieu's vehement orthodoxy. As so often, the Dutch regents had made no heroic declarations of impressive-sounding ideals; they simply permitted all comers to live in the Republic unmolested.

III THE BEGINNINGS OF DECLINE?

THE DUTCH AS A GREAT POWER

In the second half of the seventeenth century the Dutch Republic was unquestionably one of the European great powers, whether under the leadership of the Pensionary Johan de Witt (from 1653 to 1672) or of William III (from 1672 to 1702).

The two men – tragically rivals because of the events of 1650 – were alike in their dedication to what they believed to be the interests of their country, in their capacity for hard work and unremitting attention to detail, and in their skill in manipulating the complex Dutch institutions and factions to suit their purposes. In other respects they were very dissimilar. De Witt was the son of a regent (who had been imprisoned by William II in the castle of Loevestein in 1650); he had been brought up, not for a career in commerce or finance, but for a life in the public service; he was a mathematician and a pioneer of life insurance on a scientific basis; he translated Corneille's *Horace* into Dutch; he was not particularly interested either in wealth (his salary was small, and he made little profit from his office) or in personal display. Temple noted 'his habit grave, and plain, and popular; his table, what only serv'd turn for his family, or a friend . . . he was seen usually in the streets on foot and alone, like the commonest burgher of the town.'

William, by contrast, never forgot that he was a prince, that his mother and wife were princesses, and that he stood close to the English succession. He was not self-indulgent, nor was he as extravagant as Louis XIV, but his mode of life had to be one fitting to his position, and his houses at Het Loo and Hampton Court, though not palatial like Versailles, had to contain suitable allegorical references. He enjoyed the hunt and the battlefield. His eyes were turned much more to the European scene than to the ocean lanes on which de Witt and his backers in Holland were so often intent – though the contrast is far from absolute.

In foreign policy, however, the preoccupations of both men were essentially defensive. This did not mean that their methods might

143 William III as a boy: a portrait attributed to Abraham Ragueneau.

144 Johan de Witt. Pensionary from 1653 to 1672, he was murdered during the crisis of the French invasion.

not include the dispatch of fleets to the Sound, the Tagus, the Mediterranean or the coast of Guinea to enforce settlements by vigorous action. But they were not concerned with territorial annexations. The recovery of Brazil and New Amsterdam was not a main objective of de Witt, and William did not revive the ambitions of Frederick Henry to conquer the Spanish Netherlands. The policies of both men recognized, in different ways, that the nature and the needs of the Dutch state differed from those of the continental monarchies, whose rulers wished primarily, like landowners, to expand their estates. The fleets and armies of the Republic could be used only for purposes which commended themselves to those who paid for them and whose co-operation had to be laboriously gained – in other words, to preserve the freedom of the seas (at least in European waters) and to ensure security from invasion.

The first of these aims meant constant vigilance to see that both

145 Wendela Bicker, daughter and granddaughter of burgomasters of Amsterdam, and wife of Johan de Witt.

sides of the entrance to the Baltic did not fall into the hands of a single power strong enough to interfere with the all-important 'mother-trade', and occasional demonstrations in the Mediterranean; naval war with a major power was something to be avoided if at all possible, because it risked enemy interference with the delicate web of Dutch trade, without offering any prospect of real advantages which the Dutch did not already possess. The three wars which the English call 'the Dutch wars' and the Dutch call 'the English wars' (1652–54, 1665–67 and 1672–74) were all unwelcome to the Dutch: the first two took place when they did essentially because jealous English commercial interests were able, for brief moments, to press the government to attempt to break Dutch commercial and naval strength by force.

In the first war the two sides were fairly evenly matched in battle, but the Dutch were at a serious strategic disadvantage because their

Revier

van

Rochester.

merchant shipping was exposed to attack in the Channel from English privateers. If they could not drive the English fleet from the sea and convoy the merchantmen, their only recourse was the hazardous journey round the north of Scotland, and there still remained the possibility of attack in the North Sea. There were always more Dutch than English ships to be taken as prizes, and before long the trade of Amsterdam was suffering severely. It was the memory of this situation which led de Witt to devote more resources to building up the navy than the army, and which incited the English to make another attempt in 1665.

This time the fighting again produced no decisive result, but Dutch trade had more protection and Dutch money lasted longer than that of Charles II. In 1667 de Witt brought the war to a hasty conclusion by sending de Ruyter's fleet into the Medway to wreak havoc on the English ships. Resistance was small, but this famous event was a remarkable feat of seamanship and daring in treacherous channels. As a result, the Treaty of Breda allowed the Dutch to end the war without making any significant concessions. They promised to salute

146 The raid on the Medway, 10–13 June 1667: de Ruyter and his fleet attack English ships moored at Rochester and Chatham.

147 The captured *Royal Charles* reaches the River Maas.

the British flag in 'British waters', but they were too businesslike to bother as much about points of precedence as the English and French, provided that their commercial and fishing interests were safeguarded. They did agree that the New Netherlands (which had been captured by the English and rechristened New York) should be exchanged for Surinam; but neither party to the Treaty then appreciated how important New York was later to become.

At about the same time, however, the Dutch also faced danger from another quarter. Their relations with France had been friendly since the time of their alliance with Henry of Navarre, but already in the 1630s there had been those who would rather see *Gallum amicum quam vicinum* and disliked the possibility of France swallowing up the Spanish Netherlands. In 1668 de Witt took measures to restrict Louis XIV's conquests from Spain in the 'War of Devolution', and Louis realized that if he was to make further gains he must first knock out the Dutch.

This was Louis's principal motive for attacking the Dutch in 1672; Charles II of England joined him to avenge the disgrace of the Medway. The Dutch were powerless to prevent Louis XIV from marching into the heart of the Republic and establishing himself at Utrecht, and for several months the independence of the United Provinces (and consequently the whole of north-west Europe) from Bourbon domination hung on the maintenance of the 'water line' of flooded land in front of the cities of the province of Holland, while the combined English and French fleets threatened invasion from the sea. At the same time the urban populations turned to William of Orange for salvation, and in an atmosphere of crisis and rioting de Witt was first obliged to resign, and was then lynched, and his body mutilated, by a mob in the Hague. This gruesome episode showed that beneath the apparently smooth surface of Dutch society ugly passions seethed. Orangists were active at the time, and although William was probably ignorant of what precisely was being planned, he rewarded some of them afterwards. He was a young, inexperienced man, eager for power to save his country, and, as on some later occasions, he believed that he who was not against him was for him – and deserved reward.

The events of 1672 were a traumatic experience for the Dutch. They did not emerge from them with deep resentment against the English: de Ruyter's fleet had saved them from invasion, commerce had been preserved from the disorganization which had taken place in

148 The murder of the brothers Cornelis and Johan de Witt: detail from the print by Romeyn de Hooghe.

1653, and early in 1674 Charles II abandoned the war under pressure from his Parliament. But the atrocities of Louis XIV's armies, and the harsh terms that he had sought to impose, were long remembered, especially when Huguenot refugees from his rule arrived, and when Louis was responsible for further aggression. In three long wars from 1672 to 1678, 1689 to 1697 and 1702 to 1713, the Dutch were at the centre of anti-French coalitions, formed by the unremitting effort of William III. Their quest for security eventually crystallized into a desire to garrison a line of barrier fortresses in Flanders which would prevent another dramatic French invasion like that of 1672.

By the time of the Treaty of Utrecht in 1713 this aim had been achieved, and the Republic, together with Great Britain and western Europe generally, was safe from French aggression for some time to come. But the effort had taken a severe toll. The three wars were far more costly than the campaigns against Spain a century earlier, and, in spite of the excellent credit facilities, very heavy taxation was necessary. The nature of the Dutch war effort also changed. It is noticeable that in the last two of the wars, which were fought in alliance with Britain, the Dutch contribution to the joint fleet became steadily smaller in proportion to the British one; and still the five Dutch admiralties found it difficult to have their ships ready as promised. In the 1690s William was not unwilling to let his English subjects take the lead at sea, while Dutch resources helped to provide him with larger armies to lead on land. In the War of the Spanish Succession, Marlborough's battles, commonly regarded as British victories, were won with coalition armies, containing comparatively few British troops: the Dutch contribution was indispensable, and the Dutch deputies who travelled with Marlborough were reluctant to allow him to fight costly battles, because they knew that if the army were destroyed it would be almost impossible to replace it.

When, therefore, the Dutch had achieved security (as they thought) by gaining their barrier, any desire for military glory was fully slaked. They still had an interest in restoring peace in the Baltic, and in maintaining the Utrecht settlement from disturbance, but they had no prince to involve them in any military adventures for the conquest of territory. At the time of the War of the Polish Succession, Walpole made a famous boast that in the slaughter not a single Englishman was involved. The Dutch could have made the same boast, and at the time of the Seven Years' War they could have repeated it, except that their ships suffered from English searches.

It is, in the first place, this relative inactivity after 1720 which leads historians to speak in terms of 'Dutch decline'. Historians are naturally politically minded, and tend to move states up and down league tables according to the power which they can deploy on the international scene. By these standards there can be no doubt that in the early eighteenth century the Dutch began a decline from the position that they had occupied in the previous century. Yet the benefits of neutrality, however 'inglorious', are not negligible, and it was not until 1780 that military weakness had serious consequences.

149 Earthenware punch-bowl commemorates the Peace of Rijswijk, 1697.

150, 151 The Six family contributed burgomasters in the seventeenth and eighteenth centuries: (left) Rembrandt's portrait of Jan Six in 1654, and (right) his eighteenth-century successor, also named Jan Six, by Arnold Boonen.

ECONOMIC AND SOCIAL PROBLEMS

In the same way, when we speak of economic decline, we mean essentially that Dutch trade no longer excited the jealousy of other nations as it had done in the middle of the seventeenth century. For a long time, however, this was not because the Dutch share in European and world trade had shrunk in absolute terms, but because the total volume of trade had grown, and England and France had been able to find scope for expansion in the Indian Ocean, the West Indies and the Mediterranean without further commercial wars against the Dutch. In the Baltic, which the Dutch had once monopolized, direct trade grew between France and the countries of the north and east; and the shipping of the Scandinavian countries and of Hamburg increased. But this did not mean that Dutch commercial activity generally decreased: on the contrary, there were marked spurts in the concluding years of the seventeenth century, and again after the Utrecht and Nystadt settlements had restored peace to Europe. In some areas there was considerable growth, for instance in the sugar, coffee and cocoa plantations in Surinam. At the beginning of the eighteenth century Dutch-built ships were still in demand from foreign owners; it was still to the shipyards of the Zaan that Peter the Great came to learn his carpenter's trade. In 1707 there were 306 ships on the stocks. In 1721, 257 whalers were sent out to Arctic waters, only seven fewer than the peak figure attained in 1684.

Nevertheless, the competitive position of Dutch commerce did become weaker in the eighteenth century, and in some industries, notably the cloth industry at Leiden, the fall in production was steep. Any attempt to work this out in detail and to examine its causes and rate would lead us too far beyond the end of our period. Suffice it to say that recent research suggests both that the decline came later than was once thought, and that the economic problems faced by the Dutch cannot any longer be explained simply in 'moral' terms, as though it was a matter of the degeneracy of the eighteenth-century regents from their vigorous, enterprising and progressive seventeenth-century predecessors. The character of the patrician class was changing, but in the first place the significance of the change was social rather than economic.

The city oligarchies had become even more exclusive. The city of Amsterdam came to be dominated by three families only, especially that of Johan Corver, who held a great feast in 1716 to celebrate fifty years on the city council. Between 1696 and 1748 forty new burgomasters were chosen: only three of these were not related to previous burgomasters, and those three held office only briefly. In all the towns, 'contracts of correspondence' became more common: these were agreements by the leading families to share power and to take turns in the highest offices. The practice could be defended as a means of bringing about harmony within the town councils; but the drawback was that, though friction was reduced, the possibility of ventilating different points of view and policies was reduced too. Thanks to agreements, intermarriage and the evasion of clauses in charters which were designed to prevent the excessive concentration of power in a few hands, the councils were occupied more and more by an élite of wealthy people, who were *rentiers* rather than active businessmen, and who sought more profitable investments in other countries (notably England, after the foundation of the Bank in 1694) rather than in their own.

Contemporaries began to notice a more and more ostentatious style of living: Carr's descriptions in 1688 already differ markedly from Temple's observations in 1672. The change can be seen in the paintings of the second half of the seventeenth century – compare for instance, Pieter de Hooch's later paintings with his earlier ones. The silks and velvets of the sitters became more expensive. The *pronkstilleven* contained ever costlier china, silverware and tablecloths. The houses on the Amsterdam canals (like the Trippenhuis, though admittedly that was intended for two families) became larger, more classical, made of stone rather than brick, and with more furniture, marble and gilt inside; servants became more numerous. This tendency for consumption to become even more conspicuous was not peculiar to the Netherlands – it was common to the wealthier classes all over Europe in the last quarter of the seventeenth century – but its social consequences were especially serious there. The gap between the rich and the poor (under their burden of indirect taxation) became steadily wider.

It was even true that the regents, who had previously had an ambivalent attitude to the established church, began to draw closer to it, so that another source of creative tension was stopped. Preachers were less critical of the luxury of the regents; the regents, who had previously included a significant proportion of Remonstrants and others, belonged more and more to the Calvinist church, served as elders in it and were politely received as commissioners in its synods.

The extent to which these trends had developed by the time of the Treaty of Utrecht in 1713 should not be exaggerated, but they were ominous for the future, because they made for rule by a conservative, self-satisfied oligarchy which was content to continue in the same old ways and to avoid all risks. As long as Dutch fortunes progressed smoothly, these social and political institutions would be enough to guarantee a degree of peace, prosperity and intellectual freedom sufficient to arouse the envy of some other less fortunate peoples; but when important reforms and changes of direction were necessary, they would not prove to be easily adaptable. The possibility of enlightened administrative, legal and social reform would be smothered by the weight of custom and the difficulty of taking initiatives. No new government policy, whether in taxation or tariffs, brought effective aid to Leiden. The greatest Dutch economic successes in the eighteenth century were not to be in developing new and adventurous commercial lines or industries, but in the operations of the Amsterdam money market (which retained its importance down to the French Revolution), and in trade in colonial produce from the East and West Indies.

Differences of opinion may be possible about the rate of political and economic decline, whether relative or absolute, but there can be no argument about the decline in the standard of Dutch painting in the last fifty years of our period. It would have been extraordinary if the standard could have been maintained; it may perhaps be thought that the essential characteristics of Dutch painting were not ones which were capable of indefinite refinement and development. The flower-pieces of Jan van Huysum (1682–1749) were extremely skilful, but scarcely deserved higher prices than the works of earlier and greater painters. The career of Gerard de Lairesse (1641–1711), with his academic, classical and allegorical approach to decoration, and his extremely influential lectures on theory, shows the loss of the original spontaneity; and the fact that Adriaen van der Werff (1659–1722) got higher prices than Rembrandt reflects badly on the taste of the period, though it is partly attributable to the scarcity of good new paintings at a time when more money was available for their purchase.

152, 153 The late seventeenth and eighteenth centuries brought increasing intricacy and ornament to the arts: (left) a tulip-holder from the Blue Delft period, and (right) van Huysum's *Flowerpiece* (1726).

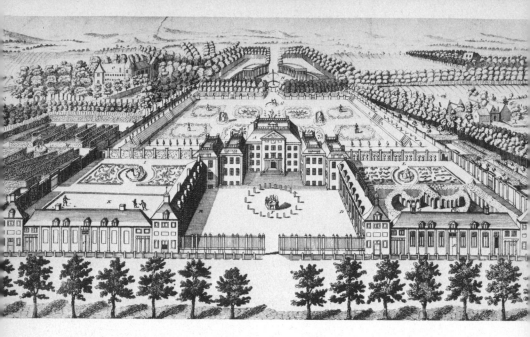

In another area, however, Dutch artists were more successful – in the production of Delftware of all kinds. The best period of Blue Delft began about 1680, and the potters produced some beautiful works of art which were something more than mere imitation of Chinese porcelain. Greater technical skill also enabled them to produce some works which were more remarkable for their ingenuity than for their beauty – tulip-vases, violins, bird-cages and so on. The patronage of William and Mary at Hampton Court no doubt did a great deal to stimulate the interest of English collectors, and many fine Dutch tiles and pieces of Blue Delft entered English country houses in the next generation.

In many ways the most significant artist of the late seventeenth and early eighteenth centuries was Daniel Marot (1663–1752). One of the many Huguenots who came to the Dutch Republic in the 1680s, he was employed by William III in the construction, ornamentation and furnishing of his houses at Het Loo and elsewhere, and afterwards by other rich patrons in The Hague and Amsterdam. In comparison with later work, much of what he did probably seems heavy, overloaded with gilding and more luxurious than graceful; yet these faults are widespread in the period, and by no means confined either to the Dutch or to Marot. At its best, as in the Trêveszaal at

156 Right: Delft jar
of about 1690,
with Chinese pattern.

154 Opposite:
prospect of
William III's palace
at Het Loo.

155 Below: William and Mary,
a portrait by the
English miniaturist,
Peter Hoadly.

157 Right: Blue Delft tile
with portrait of
William III
on horseback,
a design after
Daniel Marot.

The Hague (1696–98), in which the States-General received foreign ambassadors, his work is attractive as well as impressive. Sometimes it has been too severely criticized as an example of the abandonment of the simplicity of native Dutch taste under the influence of French models. This can be seen, not only in the ornamentation and furnishing inside the houses, but also in the gardens which were planned for Het Loo, and which abandoned the characteristic Dutch garden in favour of terraces, statues and waterworks derived from Versailles.

French influences and tastes had always been strong, particularly at the courts of the princes of Orange, where the French language was spoken. The famous last words of the patriot William the Silent, uttered after he had been shot on the stairs of the Prinsenhof at Delft – 'Ayez pitié de mon âme et de ce pauvre peuple' – were in French, not Dutch. In the 1630s Frederick Henry, whose mother was Louise de Coligny, and who received the title of *Altesse* from Richelieu, set to work deliberately to build up his household into a court in a French style; his houses at Honselaersdijk and Rijswijk were French-inspired. William III, the great enemy of Louis XIV, spoke and wrote French (though his orthography left much to be desired), and the plan for Het Loo may have come from the Académie d'Architecture at Paris.

But as the seventeenth century progressed, the French language and French fashions became more widespread, even outside the court circle. The very needs of Dutch trade made it more necessary for Dutchmen than other peoples to be able to speak foreign languages, and contemporaries admired their facility in this, as they still do today. 'By reason of the Flemings' general skill in strange languages', wrote one, 'strangers may pass and trade among them though they cannot speak a word of the vulgar tongue.' French was the most widely taught of these languages. After all, before the Revolt, Dutch- and French-speaking people had lived side by side in the southern Netherlands, and after it the famous influx of Walloon immigrants into the North, with their Walloon congregations and important place in social and economic life, provided an obvious stimulus. When the practice developed of sending the sons of regent families on a kind of Grand Tour, France, with its Huguenot churches and academies as well as its other attractions, was as an obvious place to visit. Until 1672, political relations between the two countries were almost continuously friendly. French books became ever more numerous; the Elseviers and other publishers began to reprint French plays, and Molière,

158 The Trêveszaal, decorated by Daniel Marot in the style of Louis XIV, illustrates the influence of France, imported by Huguenot refugees.

Corneille and Racine began to oust Breero and other Dutch play-wrights from the theatres favoured by the well-to-do and the fashion-able.

From 1672, relations between the two governments moved from friendship to hostility, but paradoxically the penetration of French cultural influences became deeper as a result of the arrival of the Huguenots. Whereas those who sought refuge in England soon found it indispensable to learn English if they were to make their way, those who went to Holland found many who could speak French and even join in worship in their Walloon churches. Bayle, for instance, found it possible to spend a quarter of a century in Rotterdam without learning Dutch – though he could read Italian and Spanish. He could converse easily with other scholars, and publish his books in French in the knowledge that they would find a local, as well as an international, public. Others who earned a living by more mundane pursuits must have found it more urgent to learn Dutch, but for many intellectuals the obvious *lingua franca* literally was French.

This is particularly noticeable in the pioneering literary reviews which were founded at this time. There was a *Boekzaal*, founded in 1692, and a *Hollandsche Spectator* (1731–35); but these were less significant than the *Nouvelles de la République des Lettres* edited by Bayle from 1684 to 1687, and by others until 1718, Le Clerc's *Bibliothèque Universelle* (1689–93), *Bibliothèque Choisie* (1703–13) and *Bibliothèque Ancienne et Moderne* (1714–27), and the *Misanthrope* (1711–12) and *Journal Littéraire* (1713–22), to which Justus van Effen was the principal contributor. By developing these new media for the exchange of ideas and the discussion of books, Dutch publishers were rendering an inestimable service to the intellectual life of western Europe; but the journals were written in French, not in Dutch.

To patriotic Dutch historians like Professor Geyl, this is a matter for deep regret. Earlier in the century writers like Vondel and Hooft had produced great poetry and prose literature, written in the vernacular. Their successors produced work in French which was highly derivative. The writings of Justus van Effen, the best of the Dutch-born authors (who used both French and Dutch), were respectable but lacking in originality. In art and fashion too, the old native inspiration was submerged by the same foreign, and particularly French, influences. In all this a good deal of social and cultural snobbery was inevitably involved.

One cannot but feel sympathy for this attitude towards the end of the great period of Dutch creativity. Yet the foreign observer may also feel, not only that these features were an unavoidable consequence of the position that the Dutch occupied, but that at least for Europe as a whole there were some compensations. The Dutch were always a small people with an open society, exposed by its very commercial nature to contact with innumerable influences from other larger societies. They could not possibly have maintained a cultural exclusiveness, even if that had been a wholly healthy thing. The smaller languages must always have a hard struggle against the pull of the larger; and it would have been a strange blindness, in a great international centre of civilization, which failed to recognize the achievements of French culture in the seventeenth and eighteenth centuries.

The compensation was the part which the Dutch were able to play in the transmission of ideas, thanks to their intellectual freedom and their unrivalled facilities for the production of books. They not only provided a home and a publisher for people like Bayle; their journals and their printing-presses spread the works of writers of other countries to a wider international public. For instance, it appears that until about 1700 English literature, unlike the works of the classic French authors, was virtually unknown on the Continent. But in a generation in which the Dutch and English were allies, and visits more frequent than they had ever been before, this situation changed. William Sewell, whose mother was Dutch and whose grandfather was an English Brownist sectary – and who claimed to be a Dutchman himself – conducted the *Boekzaal*, translated Burnet and other authors, and prepared an English-Dutch dictionary. Van Effen, having visited England, diffused a knowledge of his visits in various ways besides imitating the *Tatler* and *Spectator* in the French *Misanthrope* and translating Swift and Defoe into French. Perhaps most important of all, it was essentially through the Netherlands that the ideas of Locke and Newton became European property. If Voltaire visited Leiden to consult Herman Boerhaave about his health, he also discussed with William Jacob 's Gravesande the physics of Newton.

The Netherlands was a great cultural crossroads, a market for the buying and selling of ideas and books as well as corn, spices, sugar and fish. The life of a community which turns itself into a great market centre cannot remain unaffected by the change: but if it loses some of its old distinctiveness and charm, it helps to meet the essential needs of others, while maintaining by no means negligible standards of civilization for itself.

IV CONCLUSION:
COSMOPOLITAN AND LOCAL

Within about a century the seven provinces which had entered into the loosest of confederations in the Union of Utrecht had developed into a coherent state. They had won their independence from Spain, and had defended the Republic against attempts to reduce it to either a French or an English protectorate in 1672. The Republic was clearly marked off from its neighbours (including the Southern Netherlands with which the provinces had been combined under the Habsburgs), and it was not likely to dissolve into its component parts, as some had feared in 1618. There was a unity based on common experience, on political and economic success, and on the creation of a distinctive civilization.

The state which had thus come into existence was full of paradoxes. It was a Republic, but contained one family of princes who took their name from the south of France and married into the royal House of Stuart. Its 'United Provinces' had very little in the way of common institutions or centralized bureaucracy. Its ideal was peaceful trade, and yet it was almost continually engaged in war – and often traded with the enemy. Its society included brokers who frequented the Exchange in Amsterdam and sailors and adventurers who travelled to the ends of the earth. It produced freebooters who preyed on enemy shipping, and it cultivated the domestic virtues – sometimes in the same person: there is something characteristic in the career of Klaas Compaan of Zaandam, 'the terror of the seas', who ended his days living peacefully with his wife in their small brick house in Oostzaan. It officially recognized only Calvinist worship, but in practice it indulged Catholics, Jews and a variety of sectaries. Its rulers were relatively tolerant and liberal, but based their enlightenment on no declarations of general principles.

Such contrasts could be multiplied, but one of the most significant lies in the ability to reconcile worldwide interests with an intense localism. The Dutch had contacts, and often relatives, in every country, and were particularly well supplied with news and information of every kind, and yet this cosmopolitan outlook was rooted in local pride. It was vital to know whether a Dutchman was an Amsterdammer or a Leidenaar or a Haarlemmer. If he was a townsman, he belonged to a fairly tightly-knit community, with its jealously guarded local customs, privileges and traditions, with its common concern for the maintenance of dykes and canals, its civic guards, its orphanages and almshouses, its council and its delegation voting as a body in the provincial States. Such a sense of community might transcend differences of religion among neighbours, and, though there might be disagreements, factions and even occasional crises, as in 1618 and 1672, it could hinder them from deteriorating into civil war. At the same time the Dutch showed themselves capable of encouraging immigration and assimilating immigrants when an enlightened view of the general civic interest (as well as humanity) seemed to demand it. In the villages, which had an equally strong sense of community, there was more likely to be exclusiveness and homogeneity of religious belief. But in expanding towns which depended on trade and industry the regents realized their interest in permitting whosoever would to come, in protecting them from interference by an oppressive state or church or from extradition by a foreign power, and in allowing them to hold and express any opinions which did not immediately disturb public order. Since they were masters in their own city under the very loosely organized constitution of the Republic, the regents were usually able to control the conditions under which their citizens lived.

There were blots on this record, notably in the time of the disputes between Remonstrants and Counter-Remonstrants and again in the riots of the crisis-year of 1672. Nevertheless, the *Observations* which Sir William Temple wrote down in that same year, when the Dutch state was on the verge of ruin, contain some impressive compliments. He was not an unqualified admirer of everything he saw; he detested the Dutch climate (which he thought led to rheumatism and toothache) and much preferred his beloved English countryside.

> And indeed their country is a much better mistress than a wife; and where few persons who are well at home, would be content to live; but where none that have time to spare, would not for once be willing to travel; and as England shows, in the beauty of the country, what nature can arrive at; so does Holland, in the number, greatness and beauty of their towns, whatever art can bring to pass.

But Temple had seen his own country torn by disputes between Anglicans and Puritans, and the eventual reimposition of conformity and censorship under the Restoration; and on this point in particular, though he made no explicit comparison, he was in no doubt about the superiority of the Dutch system.

> It is hardly to be imagined, how all the violence and sharpness, which accompanies the differences of religion in other countries, seems to be appeased or softened here, by the general freedom which all men enjoy, either by allowance or connivance. . . .

And, in a later passage, he went on to say,

> No man having any reason to complain of oppression in conscience; and no man having hopes, by advancing his religion, to form a party . . . the differences in opinion make some in affections, and little in conversation. . . . They argue without interest or anger; they differ without enmity or scorn; and they agree without confederacy. Men live together, like citizens of the world, associated by the common ties of humanity, and by the bonds of peace, under the impartial protection of indifferent laws, with equal encouragement of all arts and industry, and equal freedom of speculation and enquiry.

When all due reservations have been made, it remains a significant tribute to the inhabitants of the new brick houses on the tree-lined quays of the towns whose beauty Temple admired.

CHRONOLOGY

1555	Accession of Philip II of Spain as ruler over the seventeen provinces of the Netherlands.
1568	Revolt crushed by Alva, Spanish military governor, followed by a reign of terror against rebels and heretics.
1572	Capture of Brill by the Sea Beggars, followed by a revolt in other places in Holland and Zeeland.
1574	Failure of the Spaniards at the siege of Leiden.
1575	Foundation of Leiden University.
1578	In a *coup* known as the *Alteratie*, the city of Amsterdam goes over to the rebels.
1579	Union of Utrecht, eventually joined by the seven northern provinces.
1581	Act of Abjuration, renouncing the authority of Philip II.
1584	Assassination of William I of Orange ('the Silent') at Delft.
1585	Recapture of Antwerp by the Spaniards under Parma.
1588	Defeat of the Armada.
1590	William's second son Maurice of Nassau (stadholder of Holland and Zeeland since 1585) becomes stadholder of Utrecht, Overijssel and Gelderland.
1590–94	Maurice captures Breda, Nijmegen, Groningen and other places.
1602	Foundation of the Dutch East Indies Company.
1609–21	Twelve Years' Truce with Spain.
1618–19	Synod of Dort.
1619	Trial and execution of the Advocate, Oldenbarnevelt.
1620	Departure of the 'Pilgrim Fathers' from Holland.
1621	Resumption of war with Spain and foundation of the Dutch West India Company.
1625–26	Foundation of New Amsterdam on Manhattan Island.
1625	Publication of Grotius's *De jure belli ac pacis*.
1625	Recapture of Breda by the Spaniards (cf. the painting by Velazquez).

1625	Death of Maurice, and succession of his brother Frederick Henry as stadholder.
1628	Capture of the Silver Fleet by Piet Hein off the coast of Cuba.
1628	Capture of 's Hertogenbosch and other military successes of Frederick Henry.
1632	Rembrandt's *Anatomy Lesson of Dr Tulp*.
1637	Recapture of Breda.
1639	Naval battle in the Downs, in which Tromp defeats the Spaniards.
1641	Marriage of Frederick Henry's son William to Mary, daughter of Charles I of England.
1647	Death of Frederick Henry and succession of William II as stadholder of five provinces.
1648	Recognition of Dutch independence in the Treaty of Münster.
1650	William II's attempt to capture Amsterdam, followed by his death and the birth of a son, later William III.
1650–72	First 'stadholderless period' (except in Friesland and Groningen).
1652–54	First Anglo-Dutch war, ending in the Treaty of Westminster.
1653–72	Johan de Witt Grand Pensionary of Holland.
1664	New Amsterdam seized by the English and renamed New York.
1665–67	Second Anglo-Dutch war, ending in the raid on the Medway by the Dutch fleet under de Ruyter and the Treaty of Breda.
1667–68	Invasion of the Spanish Netherlands by Louis XIV in the 'War of Devolution'.
1669	Death of Rembrandt.
1670	Publication of Spinoza's *Tractatus theologico-politicus*.
1670	Secret Treaty of Dover between Charles II and Louis XIV, providing for a joint attack on the Dutch.
1672	Outbreak of the third Anglo-Dutch war: invasion of the Republic by a French army; William III raised to power in the time of crisis; lynching of the brothers de Witt.
1674	War with England ends at the Treaty of Westminster.

1677	Marriage of William III to Mary, daughter of James, Duke of York.
1678	War with France ends at the Treaty of Nijmegen.
1685	James II succeeds in England. Persecution of Huguenots in France (culminating in the Revocation of the Edict of Nantes) leads to a large-scale emigration to the Dutch Republic.
1688	William sails to intervene in England.
1689	William and Mary become King and Queen of England.
1689–97	'War of the League of Augsburg' (or 'War of the English Succession') ending in the Treaty of Rijswijk.
1701	Formation of the 'Grand Alliance' against Louis XIV.
1702	Death of William III and beginning of the second 'stadholderless period' (lasting until 1747).
1702–13	War of the Spanish Succession, ending at the Treaty of Utrecht.

BIBLIOGRAPHY

This bibliography has been deliberately restricted to works available in English and French. Those who can read Dutch and are in search of more specialized books are referred to H. de Buck, *Bibliografie der Geschiedenis van Nederland* (Leiden 1968). Each volume of the *Algemene Geschiedenis der Nederlanden*, ed. J. A. van Houtte, J. F. Niermeyer, J. Presser, etc. (Utrecht 1949–58; vol. v, *1567–1609*; vol. vi, *1609–1648*; vol. vii, *1648–1748*) has bibliographical appendices related to each chapter of the text.

GENERAL AND POLITICAL

The best general account available in English is that of P. Geyl, *The Revolt of the Netherlands, 1555–1609* (London 1932, reprinted 1962); *The Dutch in the Seventeenth Century*, vol. i *1609–48* (London 1936, reprinted 1961), vol. ii, *1648–1715* (London 1964). This is the work of a great historian; but it is the translation of a work originally intended for Dutch readers. It takes for granted much that English readers would like to know about Dutch institutions; and Geyl's interests did not lie in economic history, which must be studied elsewhere. Geyl's view of the split between North and South has recently been forcefully challenged by Charles Wilson, *Queen Elizabeth and the Dutch Revolt* (London 1970); cf. also Sir George Clark's Raleigh Lecture, 'The Birth of the Dutch Republic', in the *Proceedings of the British Academy* (London 1946), pp. 189–217, reprinted in *Studies in History*, ed. Lucy S. Sutherland (London 1966), and J. W. Smit, 'The Present Position of Studies Regarding the Revolt of the Netherlands', in *Britain and the Netherlands* (see below) vol. i, pp. 11–28.

C. R. Boxer, *The Dutch Seaborne Empire 1600–1800* (London 1965), is not a narrative but a collection of excellent essays, mainly on the theme of maritime and commercial expansion. Charles Wilson, *The Dutch Republic and the Civilisation of the Seventeenth Century* (London 1968), is mainly concerned with the influence of the Dutch example upon the rest of Europe, particularly England.

J. Huizinga, *Dutch Civilisation in the Seventeenth Century* (Eng. trans. London 1968), is a justly famous essay. P. Zumthor, *Daily Life in*

Rembrandt's Holland (Eng. trans. London 1962), has much of interest.

C. V. Wedgwood, *William the Silent* (London 1944), is the best English biography of that statesman, but readers of German may refer to the older and more detailed work of F. Rachfahl, *Wilhelm von Oranien und der niederländische Aufstand* (3 vols. Halle and The Hague 1906–24). The best biography in English of his great-grandson is Stephen Baxter, *William III* (London 1966); but in his anxiety to establish the greatness of his hero the author is less than just to his Dutch opponents, and he has been severely criticized by Dutch historians on this account. There is no adequate account in English of any of the intervening princes of Orange or of de Witt, but the gap is partly filled by a translation of another work by P. Geyl, *Orange and Stuart* (London 1969), covering the period 1641–72.

The proceedings of three Anglo-Netherlands conferences of historians have been published in *Britain and the Netherlands*, ed. J. S. Bromley and E. H. Kossmann (vol. 1 London 1960, vol. II Groningen 1964), and *Britain and the Netherlands in Europe and Asia* (same editors, London 1968); they contain valuable articles on many themes. The new periodical *Acta Historiae Neerlandica* has English summaries of the work of Dutch historians.

The following deal with particular aspects of Dutch society.

ECONOMIC HISTORY

V. Barbour, *Capitalism in Amsterdam in the Seventeenth Century* (Baltimore 1950).
——, 'Dutch and English Merchant Shipping in the Seventeenth Century', reprinted in *Essays in Economic History*, ed. E. M. Carus-Wilson (London 1954), pp. 227–53.
A. E. Christensen, *Dutch Trade to the Baltic about 1600* (Copenhagen 1941).
D. W. Davies, *A Primer of Dutch Seventeenth-century Overseas Trade* (The Hague 1961).
J. G. van Dillen, 'The Bank of Amsterdam', in van Dillen, *History of the Principal Public Banks* (The Hague 1934), pp. 79–123.
K. Glamann, *Dutch-Asiatic Trade, 1620–1740* (The Hague 1958).
N. W. Posthumus, *Inquiry into the History of Prices in Holland* (Leiden 1946–64).
Charles Wilson, *Anglo-Dutch Commerce and Finance in the Eighteenth century* (2nd ed. Cambridge 1966).

Charles Wilson, 'The Decline of the Netherlands' and 'Taxation and the Decline of Empires, an Unfashionable Theme' in *Economic History and the Historian*, pp. 22–47 and 114–27.

For the rivalry with England, see C. Wilson, *Profit and Power. A Study of the Dutch Wars* (London 1957). Cf. also T. W. Fulton, *The Sovereignty of the Sea* (Edinburgh and London 1911); P. J. Blok, *Life of Admiral de Ruyter* (Eng. trans. London 1933); P. G. Rogers, *The Dutch in the Medway* (London 1970). G. N. Clark, *The Dutch Alliance and the War against French Trade, 1689–97* (Manchester 1923), deals with a different set of maritime and commercial problems in a later war.

RELIGION

A. W. Harrison, *The Beginnings of Arminianism* (London 1926).

D. Nobbs, *Theocracy and Toleration* (Cambridge 1938).

I. Schöffer, 'Protestantism in Flux during the Revolt of the Netherlands', in *Britain and the Netherlands* (see above), vol. II, pp. 67–83.

A. C. Carter, *The English Reformed Church in Amsterdam in the Seventeenth Century* (Amsterdam 1964).

P. Dibon, 'Le Réfuge Wallon précurseur du Réfuge Huguenot', in *XVIIe Siècle* (1967), pp. 53–74.

C. Weiss, *Histoire des Réfugis Protestants de France* (Paris 1853).

INTELLECTUAL LIFE

A. G. H. Bachrach, *Sir Constantine Huygens and Britain* (Leiden 1962).

R. Colie, *Light and Enlightenment* (Cambridge 1957).

F. Dahl, *Dutch Corantos, 1618–1650* (The Hague 1946).

D. W. Davies, *The World of the Elseviers* (The Hague 1954).

J. A. van Dorsten, *Poets, Patrons and Professors* (Leiden 1962).

W. S. M. Knight, *The Life and Works of Hugo Grotius* (London 1925).

E. Labrousse, *Pierre Bayle* (The Hague 1963).

W. J. B. Pienaar, *English Influences in Dutch Literature and Justus van Effen as Intermediary* (Cambridge 1929).

P. R. Sellin, *Daniel Heinsius and Stuart England* (Leiden-London 1968).

C. Serrurier, *Pierre Bayle en Hollande* (Apeldoorn 1912).

SCIENCE

A. G. H. Bachrach, 'Holland and Britain in the Age of Observation', in *The Orange and the Rose* (Catalogue to the exhibition at the Victoria and Albert Museum, London 1964).

A. E. Bell, *Christian Huygens and the Development of Science in the Seventeenth Century* (London 1947).

C. Dobell, *Antony van Leeuwenhoek and his 'Little Animals'* (London 1932).

G. A. Lindeboom, *Hermann Boerhaave* (London 1968).

A. Schierbeek, *Measuring the Invisible World* (London and New York 1959).

——, *Jan Swammerdam* (Amsterdam 1967).

E. G. R. Taylor, *The Haven Finding Art* (London 1956).

THE ARTS

H. E. van Gelder, *Guide to Dutch Art* (The Hague 1961).

J. G. van Gelder, *Dutch Drawings and Prints* (London 1959).

R. van Luttervelt, *The Rijksmuseum and other Dutch Museums* (London 1967).

N. Maclaren, *The Dutch School* (National Gallery Cat., London 1960).

J. Rosenberg, S. Slive and E. H. ter Kuile, *Dutch Art and Architecture 1600–1800* (Harmondsworth 1966).

W. S. Heckscher, *The Anatomy of Dr. Nicholas Tulp* (New York 1958).

J. W. Frederiks, *Dutch Silver* (4 vols. The Hague 1952–61).

K. Fremantle, *The Baroque Town Hall of Amsterdam* (Utrecht 1959).

G. L. Burke, *The Making of Dutch Towns* (London 1956).

C. H. de Jonge, *Dutch Ceramics* (London 1970).

A. Lane, *A Guide to the Collection of Tiles* (Victoria and Albert Museum Catalogue, London 1960).

SOME SEVENTEENTH-CENTURY OBSERVERS OF THE DUTCH

Sir William Temple, *Observations upon the United Provinces of the Netherlands* (ed. G. N. Clark, Cambridge 1932).

W. Carr, *Remarks of the Government . . . more particularly of the United Provinces . . .* (Amsterdam 1688. Later editions under different titles).

Jean de Parival, *Les Délices de la Hollande* (Leiden 1662).

See also: W. Brereton, *Travels in Holland . . . 1634–35*, ed. E. Hawkins (Chetham Soc., Manchester 1844); James Howell, *Epistolae Ho-elianae*, ed. J. Jacobs (London 1890); Fynes Moryson, *Itinerary* (Glasgow 1907); *Travels of Peter Mundy*, ed. R. C. Temple (London 1924); *Life of Marmaduke Rawdon* (Camden Soc., London 1863).

LIST OF ILLUSTRATIONS

20 *Liever Turcx dan Paus*; example of a propaganda badge worn by the Sea Beggars. Nederlandsch Historisch Scheepvaart Museum, Amsterdam.

21 Medal struck at Middelburg, 1588, to commemorate the defeat of the Spanish Armada. Nederlandsch Historisch Scheepvaart Museum, Amsterdam.

22 *The Battle of Gibraltar*, 25 April 1607; painting by Cornelis van Wieringen, 1622. Nederlandsch Historisch Scheepvaart Museum, Amsterdam.

23 Naval engagement off the Downs, 21 October 1639; pen and ink drawing by Willem van de Velde the Elder (1611–93). Rijksmuseum, Amsterdam.

24 The capture of the silver fleet off Cuba; anonymous engraving of 1628. Rijksmuseum, Amsterdam.

25 Piet Hein; engraving by Willem Hondius, 1629. Nederlandsch Historisch Scheepvaart Museum, Amsterdam.

26 The West India House at Amsterdam; anonymous engraving, 1641. Rijksmuseum, Amsterdam.

27 Tromp's monument in the Oude Kerk, Delft. Rijksdienst v.d. Monumentenzorg, The Hague.

28 *Admiral Michiel de Ruyter and his family*; painting by Juriaen Jacobson, 1662. Rijksmuseum, Amsterdam.

29 Windmill for draining the Beemster polder; pen and ink drawing by Jan Leeghwater, 1638. Waterschap de Beemster, Beemster.

30 *Amsterdam in 1536*; painting by Cornelis Anthonisz (*c.* 1499–*c.* 1553). Historisch Museum de Waag, Amsterdam.

31 Plan of Amsterdam; engraving from Dapper's *Historische beschryving der stadt Amsterdam*. British Museum, Department of Printed Books.

32 The cornmarket, Amsterdam; engraving from Dapper's *Historische beschryving der stadt Amsterdam*. British Museum, Department of Printed Books.

33 Commodity price list, 1674. Gemeentelijke Archiefdienst, Amsterdam.

34 Glass-blowing; engraving from Jan Luiken's *Het Menselyk Bedryf*, Amsterdam 1694. British Museum, Department of Printed Books.

35 Diamond-cutting; engraving from Luiken's *Het Menselyk Bedryf*. British Museum, Department of Printed Books.

36 Washing the fleeces and sorting the wool; painting by Isaac Swanenburgh (*c.* 1538–1614). Museum 'de Lakenhal', Leiden.

37 *View of Enkhuizen*; anonymous painting, *c.* 1600. Gemeente Enkhuizen.

38 *The Milkmaid*; engraving by Gerrit Bleker, 1643. Rijksmuseum, Amsterdam.

39 A street in Leiden; drawing on parchment, 1650. Universiteitsbibliotheek, Leiden.

40 *The Great Market at Rotterdam*; painting by Hendrik Sorgh (*c.* 1611–70). Museum Boymans-van Beuningen, Rotterdam.

41 *The Market Place and Grote Kerk at Haarlem*; painting by Gerrit Berckheyde, 1674. National Gallery, London.

42 *The Magistrates of Deventer*; painting by Gerard ter Borch, 1667. Gemeente Deventer.

43 *The Company of Frans Banningh Cocq (The Night Watch)*; painting by Rembrandt, 1672. Rijksmuseum, Amsterdam.

44 *Andries Bicker*; portrait by Bartholomeus van der Helst (1613–70). Rijksmuseum, Amsterdam.

45 *Gerard Bicker*; portrait by Bartholomeus van der Helst. Rijksmuseum, Amsterdam.

46 *Nicolaes Tulp*; portrait by Frans Hals (*c.* 1580–1666). Six Collection, Amsterdam.

47 *Diedrick Tulp*; portrait by Paulus Potter (1625–54). Six Collection, Amsterdam.

48 *Margaretha de Geer*; portrait by Rembrandt, 1661. National Gallery, London.

49 The Trippenhuis, Amsterdam. Rijksdienst v.d. Monumentenzorg, The Hague.

50 *Banquet of the Officers of the Militia Company of St George*; painting by Frans Hals, 1616. Halsmuseum, Haarlem.

51 *The Knights' Hall in the Binnenhof*, The Hague; anonymous painting, *c.* 1650. Haags Gemeentemuseum, The Hague.

52 The office of the Admiralty, Amsterdam; anonymous engraving, 1661. Rijksdienst v.d. Monumentenzorg, The Hague.

53 A *coranto* of 1633. British Museum, Department of Printed Books.

54 *The Pamphlet Seller*; engraving by Jan van der Vliet, 1630. Rijksmuseum, Amsterdam.

55 *William I of Orange*; portrait by Adriaen Key, *c.* 1578. Rijksmuseum, Amsterdam.

56 The Nassau 'Cavalcade'; engraving by Willem Delff (1580–1638). Rijksmuseum, Amsterdam.

57 Coat of arms of Prince Maurice, encircled by the Order of the Garter. Rijksmuseum, Amsterdam.

58 *Prince Maurice of Nassau at the horse fair, Valkenburg*; painting by Adriaen van de Venne (1589–1662). Rijksmuseum, Amsterdam.

59 Prince Frederick Henry of Orange; bronze plaque by Johannes Lutma senior, 1626. Rijksmuseum, Amsterdam.

60 Amalia von Solms; bronze plaque by Johannes Lutma senior, 1626. Rijksmuseum, Amsterdam.

61 *Prince Frederick Henry and Amalia von Solms*, portrait by Gerrit Honthorst (1590–1656). Mauritshuis, The Hague.

62 *Prince Maurice of Nassau*; portrait by Michiel van Miereveld (1567–1641). Rijksmuseum, Amsterdam.

63 *Prince William II*, portrait by Gerrit Honthorst. Mauritshuis, The Hague.

64 *The Prince's Birthday*; painting by Jan Steen, *c.* 1660. Rijksmuseum, Amsterdam.

65 Calvinist cartoon; anonymous engraving. Rijksmuseum, Amsterdam.

66 Verses on the Synod of Dort, and a list of delegates attending; engraving after Claes Visscher, 1639. Rijksmuseum, Amsterdam.

67 *Interior of the Grote Kerk at Haarlem*; painting by Gerrit Berckheyde, 1673. National Gallery, London.

68 *Jan Sweelinck*; portrait by Gerrit Sweelinck (1566–c. 1645), his brother. Haags Gemeentemuseum, The Hague.

69 Organ in the Nieuwe Kerk, Amsterdam. Rijksdienst v.d. Monumentenzorg, The Hague.

70 'Ons' Lieve Heer op Solder'; interior showing the high altar. Stichting Museum Amstelkring, Amsterdam.

71 Title-page of the first edition of the States' Bible, 1637. Koninklijke Bibliotheek, The Hague.

72 Cornelis Anslo; red chalk and pen drawing by Rembrandt, 1640. Louvre, Paris.

73 The Lutheran Church, Amsterdam; engraving from Dapper's *Historische beschryving der stadt Amsterdam*. British Museum, Department of Printed Books.

74 Samuel Manasseh ben Israel; portrait by Govaert Flinck, 1637. Mauritshuis, The Hague.

75 *Interior of the Portuguese Synagogue*; painting by Emanuel de Witte, 1675. Rijksmuseum, Amsterdam.

76 View of the pulpit in the Portuguese Synagogue; engraving, 1675. Universiteitsbibliotheek, Amsterdam.

77 *The Syndics of the Cloth Hall*; painting by Rembrandt, 1661. Rijksmuseum, Amsterdam.

78 *Jan van Oldenbarnevelt*; portrait by Michiel van Miereveld. Rijksmuseum, Amsterdam.

79 Jacobus Arminius; engraving from Johannes Meursius's *Athenae Batavae*, Leiden 1625. British Museum, Department of Printed Books.

80 Franciscus Gomarus; engraving from Meursius's *Athenae Batavae*. British Museum, Department of Printed Books.

81 Construction of the Remonstrant Church, Amsterdam; engraving, c. 1640. Rijksmuseum, Amsterdam.

82 Execution of Jan van Oldenbarnevelt; anonymous contemporary engraving. Photo: Mansell Collection.

83 The castle of Loevestein; anonymous engraving. Rijksmuseum, Amsterdam.

84 Hugo Grotius; engraving from Meursius's *Athenae Batavae*. British Museum, Department of Printed Books.

85 Simon Episcopius; engraving by Willem Delff. Rijksmuseum, Amsterdam.

86 John Locke; drawing by Sylvester Brownover, c. 1683. National Portrait Gallery, London.

87 *The Surrender of Breda*; painting by Velazquez, 1635. Prado, Madrid.

88 Silver salt-cellar commemorating the siege of 's Hertogenbosch, 1629, presented by Prince Frederick Henry to Pieter Jansen of Vlissingen for his courage during the siege. Rijksmuseum, Amsterdam.

89 Silver beaker showing the recapture of Breda, 1637, probably made by Schotte Jansen in 1648. Museum Boymans-van Beuningen, Rotterdam.

90 *The Surrender of the Besieged Town of Hulst to Frederick Henry*; painting by Hendrick de Meyer. Rijksmuseum, Amsterdam.

91 *The Swearing of the Oath of Ratification of the Treaty of Münster, 15 May 1648*; painting by Gerard ter Borch. By courtesy of the Trustees of the National Gallery, London.

92 *William II and Mary Stuart*; portrait by Anthony van Dyck (1599–1641). Rijksmuseum, Amsterdam.

93 *Prince William II with his army before the rebellious city of Amsterdam, August 1650*; painting by Johannes Lingelbach (1622–74). Rijksmuseum, Amsterdam.

94 The Leiden Academy; engraving from Meursius's *Athenae Batavae*. British Museum, Department of Printed Books.

95 Willibrord Snellius; engraving from Meursius's *Athenae Batavae*. British Museum, Department of Printed Books.

96 A student in his room; seventeenth-century engraving. Atlas van Stolk, Rotterdam.

97 The Botanical Garden at Leiden University; engraving from Meursius's *Athenae Batavae*. British Museum, Department of Printed Books.

98 Herman Boerhaave; drawing by Jan Wandelaar (1690–1759). Medical and Pharmaceutical Museum, Amsterdam.

99 The Anatomical Theatre at Leiden; engraving by Jacob de Gheyn II. Universiteitsbibliotheek, Leiden.

100 Title-page of William Piso's *De Indiae utriusque re naturali et medica*, published by the Elsevier Press, Amsterdam 1658. British Museum, Department of Printed Books.

101 Joost van den Vondel; pen drawing on ivory by Clemens Nachtegaal. Rijksmuseum, Amsterdam.

102 Constantijn Huygens; pen drawing on ivory by Clemens Nachtegaal. Rijksmuseum, Amsterdam.

103 Benedictus de Spinoza; anonymous portrait. Herzog August-Bibliothek, Wolfenbüttel.

104 Studies of a field mouse; pen and brush drawing by Jacob de Gheyn II. Rijksprentenkabinet, Amsterdam.

105 *Vanitas*; painting by Pieter Steenwyck. Museum 'de Lakenhal', Leiden.

106 *The Anatomy Lesson of Dr Tulp*; painting by Rembrandt, 1632. Mauritshuis, The Hague.

107 *The Love Letter*; painting by Jan Vermeer (1632–75). Rijksmuseum, Amsterdam.

108 *A Scene on the Ice*; painting by Adam van Breen, *c.* 1611. Courtesy H. Schickman Gallery, New York. Photo: Sotheby and Co.

109 *A Wooded Landscape with Cottages*; painting by Meindert Hobbema (1638–1709). Photo: Sotheby and Co.

110 *The Triumph of Frederick Henry, Prince of Orange*; painting by Jacob Jordaens (1593–1678). Koninklijk Paleis 'Huis ten Bosch', The Hague.

111 Detail of a perspective box; painting by Samuel van Hoogstraten (1627–78). National Gallery, London.

112 Diamond engraved glass with the inscription *à demain les affaires*; engraved by Anna Tesselschade. Rijksmuseum, Amsterdam.

113 Silver ewer made by Adam van Vianen, Utrecht, *c.* 1620. Rijksmuseum, Amsterdam.

114 Delft tile picture; earthenware, *c.* 1700. Rijksmuseum, Amsterdam.

115 Silver filigree clock, late seventeenth century. By courtesy of the Victoria and Albert Museum.

116 The four continents pay tribute to Amsterdam; west pediment of Amsterdam Town Hall. Photo: Stichting Lichtbeelden-Instituut, Amsterdam.

117 *The Old Town Hall, Amsterdam*; painting by Pieter Saenredam (1597–1665). Rijksmuseum, Amsterdam.

118 *The New Town Hall, Amsterdam*; painting by Jan van der Heyden (1637–1712). Louvre, Paris.

119 The Mauritshuis, The Hague. Rijksdienst v.d. Monumentenzorg, The Hague.

120 The house of Frans Banningh Cocq on the Singel, Amsterdam; anonymous drawing. De Graeff album, Rijksmuseum, Amsterdam.

121 *The Herengracht, Amsterdam*; painting by Gerrit Berckheyde. Six Collection, Amsterdam.

122 *Interior with Mother and Child*; painting by Pieter de Hooch, *c.* 1660.

123 Portrait of Simon Stevin. Universiteitsbibliotheek, Leiden.

124 Title-page of the English edition of Simon Stevin's *De Thiende*, London 1608. British Museum, Department of Printed Books.

125 Interior of the oldest preserved pendulum clock, 1657, using Christian Huygens's pendulum mechanism. Rijksmuseum voor de Geschiedenis der Natuurwetenschappen, Leiden.

126 Face of the oldest preserved pendulum clock, 1657, using Christian Huygens's pendulum mechanism. Rijksmuseum voor de Geschiedenis der Natuurwetenschappen, Leiden.

127 Spermatozoa seen by Antonie van Leeuwenhoek; engraving from Leeuwenhoek's *Opera Omnia*, Amsterdam 1719. British Museum, Department of Printed Books.

128 Microscope made by Leeuwenhoek. Science Museum, London.

129 Frontispiece of Jan Swammerdam's *De Respiratione*, Leiden 1667. British Museum, Department of Printed Books.

130 *The Lean Kitchen*; painting by Jan Steen. National Gallery of Canada, Ottawa.

131 Detail of Dutch peasantry, fisherfolk and townspeople; from Blaeu's map of of Holland, 1608. British Museum, Department of Maps.

132 The old people's home, Amsterdam; engraving from Dapper's *Historische beschryving der stadt Amsterdam*. British Museum, Department of Printed Books.

133 *The Women Governors of the Old Men's Home*; painting by Frans Hals, 1664. Halsmuseum, Haarlem.

134 The *Rasphuis*; engraving from Johannes Pontanus's *Rerum et urbis Amstelodamensium historia*, Amsterdam 1611. British Museum, Department of Printed Books.

135 Entrance of the Amsterdam bankruptcy office in the Town Hall, Amsterdam. Rijksdienst v.d. Monumentenzorg, The Hague.

136 Seventeenth-century letter showing address and stamp. Het Nederlandse Postmuseum, The Hague.

137 The differences between the old and new fire engines; engraving by Jan van der Heyden. Rijksmuseum, Amsterdam.

138 *Merry Company*; painting by Jan Steen, 1666. Mauritshuis, The Hague.

139 *Coster's Nederduitsche Academie*; engraving by Jan Philips (1700–73). Rijksmuseum, Amsterdam.

140 Children's sports; engraving by Hendrick Verstralen (1588–1635). Rijksmuseum, Amsterdam.

141 The English church, Amsterdam; engraving from Dapper's *Historische beschryving der stadt Amsterdam*. British Museum, Department of Printed Books.

142 Pierre Bayle; portrait by Carl Vanloo (1705–65). Radio Times Hulton Picture Library.

143 *William III as a boy*; portrait attributed to Abraham Ragueneau. Halsmuseum, Haarlem.

144 *Johan de Witt*; portrait by Jan de Baen (1633–1702). Rijksmuseum, Amsterdam.

145 *Wendela Bicker*; portrait by Adriaen van der Burg (1693–1733). Haags Gemeentemuseum, The Hague.

146 The Dutch fleet in the Medway, June 1667; engraving by Romeyn de Hooghe (1645–1708). Rijksmuseum, Amsterdam.

147 *The Royal Charles;* painting by Jan van Diest (1631–73). Rijksmuseum, Amsterdam.

148 Murder of Cornelis and Johan de Witt; engraving by Romeyn de Hooghe. Rijksmuseum, Amsterdam.

149 Punch-bowl commemorating the Peace of Rijswijk, 1697; enamelled buff-coloured earthenware from Delft. By courtesy of the Victoria and Albert Museum, London.

150 *Jan Six*; portrait by Rembrandt. Six Collection, Amsterdam.

151 Portrait of the eighteenth-century burgomaster, Jan Six, by Arnold Boonen (1669–1729). Six Collection, Amsterdam.

152 Tulip-holder; Delftware. By courtesy of the Victoria and Albert Museum.

153 *Flowerpiece*; painting by Jan van Huysum (1682–1749). By courtesy of the Trustees of the Wallace Collection, London.

154 A prospect of William III's palace at Het Loo. British Museum, Department of Prints and Drawings.

155 *William III and Mary*; miniature by Peter Hoadly. Rijksmuseum, Amsterdam.

156 Delft jar, *c.* 1690. Rijksmuseum, Amsterdam.

157 Blue Delft tile with portrait of William III, after Daniel Marot. Rijksmuseum, Amsterdam.

158 The Trêveszaal, The Hague. Rijksdienst v.d. Monumentenzorg, The Hague.

INDEX

Page numbers in italics refer to illustrations